THE LAB MANUAL

to accompany

Henry

THE
MASTER
READER

Third Edition

Mary Dubbé
Thomas Nelson Community College

Longman

Boston   Columbus   Indianapolis   New York   San Francisco   Upper Saddle River

Amsterdam   Cape Town   Dubai   London   Madrid   Milan   Munich   Paris   Montreal   Toronto

Delhi   Mexico City   São Paulo   Sydney   Hong Kong   Seoul   Singapore   Taipei   Tokyo

The Lab Manual to accompany Henry, *The Master Reader, Third Edition*

1 2 3 4 5 6 7 8 9 10–CW–13 12 11 10

Longman is an
imprint of

www.pearsonhighered.com

ISBN 10: 0-205-83520-1
ISBN 13: 978-0-205-83520-1

CONTENTS

About the Lab Manual: For Students ... vi
About the Lab Manual: For Instructors ... vii
About the Series ... viii
About the Lab Manual Author ... ix

Chapter 1: A Reading System for Master Readers
Lab 1.1 Practice Exercise 1 ... 1
Lab 1.2 Practice Exercise 2 ... 4
Lab 1.3 Review Test 1 ... 7
Lab 1.4 Review Test 2 ... 10
Lab 1.5 Mastery Test 1 ... 12
Lab 1.6 Mastery Test 2 ... 15

Chapter 2: Vocabulary Skills
Lab 2.1 Practice Exercise 1 ... 18
Lab 2.2 Practice Exercise 2 ... 20
Lab 2.3 Review Test 1 ... 22
Lab 2.4 Review Test 2 ... 24
Lab 2.5 Mastery Test 1 ... 26
Lab 2.6 Mastery Test 2 ... 28

Chapter 3: Stated Main Ideas
Lab 3.1 Practice Exercise 1 ... 30
Lab 3.2 Practice Exercise 2 ... 32
Lab 3.3 Review Test 1 ... 35
Lab 3.4 Review Test 2 ... 37
Lab 3.5 Mastery Test 1 ... 39
Lab 3.6 Mastery Test 2 ... 42

Chapter 4: Implied Main Ideas and Implied Central Ideas
Lab 4.1 Practice Exercise 1 ... 46
Lab 4.2 Practice Exercise 2 ... 50
Lab 4.3 Review Test 1 ... 54
Lab 4.4 Review Test 2 ... 58
Lab 4.5 Mastery Test 1 ... 62
Lab 4.6 Mastery Test 2 ... 65

Chapter 5: Supporting Details, Outlines, and Concept Maps
Lab 5.1 Practice Exercise 1 ... 69
Lab 5.2 Practice Exercise 2 ... 71
Lab 5.3 Review Test 1 ... 73
Lab 5.4 Review Test 2 ... 75
Lab 5.5 Mastery Test 1 ... 78
Lab 5.6 Mastery Test 2 ... 80

Chapter 6: Outlines and Concept Maps
Lab 6.1 Practice Exercise 1 ... 82
Lab 6.2 Practice Exercise 2 ... 84

Lab 6.3 Review Test 1   87
Lab 6.4 Review Test 2   89
Lab 6.5 Mastery Test 1   91
Lab 6.6 Mastery Test 2   93

Chapter 7: Transitions and Thought Patterns
Lab 7.1 Practice Exercise 1   95
Lab 7.2 Practice Exercise 2   97
Lab 7.3 Review Test 1   99
Lab 7.4 Review Test 2   102
Lab 7.5 Mastery Test 1   105
Lab 7.6 Mastery Test 2   107

Chapter 8: More Thought Patterns
Lab 8.1 Practice Exercise 1   109
Lab 8.2 Practice Exercise 2   113
Lab 8.3 Review Test 1   115
Lab 8.4 Review Test 2   117
Lab 8.5 Mastery Test 1   119
Lab 8.6 Mastery Test 2   121

Chapter 9: Fact and Opinion
Lab 9.1 Practice Exercise 1   124
Lab 9.2 Practice Exercise 2   126
Lab 9.3 Review Test 1   128
Lab 9.4 Review Test 2   130
Lab 9.5 Mastery Test 1   132
Lab 9.6 Mastery Test 2   134

Chapter 10: Tone and Purpose
Lab 10.1 Practice Exercise 1   136
Lab 10.2 Practice Exercise 2   138
Lab 10.3 Review Test 1   140
Lab 10.4 Review Test 2   142
Lab 10.5 Mastery Test 1   144
Lab 10.6 Mastery Test 2   147

Chapter 11: Inferences
Lab 11.1 Practice Exercise 1   150
Lab 11.2 Practice Exercise 2   153
Lab 11.3 Review Test 1   155
Lab 11.4 Review Test 2   157
Lab 11.5 Mastery Test 1   159
Lab 11.6 Mastery Test 2   161

Chapter 12: The Basics of Argument
Lab 12.1 Practice Exercise 1   163
Lab 12.2 Practice Exercise 2   166
Lab 12.3 Review Test 1   168
Lab 12.4 Review Test 2   170
Lab 12.5 Mastery Test 1   172
Lab 12.6 Mastery Test 2   174

Chapter 13: Advanced Argument: Persuasive Techniques
Lab 13.1 Practice Exercise 1   176
Lab 13.2 Practice Exercise 2   178
Lab 13.3 Review Test 1   180
Lab 13.4 Review Test 2   182

Lab 13.5 Mastery Test 1   184
Lab 13.6 Mastery Test 2   186
Practice Tests
Practice Tests for the Florida College Basic Skills Exit Reading Tests   189
Practice Tests for the Texas Higher Education Assessment Test (THEA)   191
Practice Tests for *The Master Reader*   193
Skills Awareness Inventory: Florida College Basic Skills Exit Test   195
Skills Awareness Inventory: Texas Higher Education Assessment   197
Skills Awareness Inventory: *The Master Reader*   198
Summary Sheet of Scores   201

v

For Students:

This Lab Manual is a collection of 78 activities designed to provide additional practice and enrichment for the skills in *The Master Reader*. Each chapter consists of six lab activities that can be used to add flexibility and interest to the classroom or for additional practice and for assessment purposes.

These lab activities provide students with a range of opportunities to practice becoming effective readers. The chapters of *The Master Reader* include numerous practices, applications, review tests, and mastery tests. The Lab Manual offers two practice exercises, two review tests, and two mastery tests that mirror the design of the text and emphasize the reading skills and applications students need to succeed in college. Students apply the strategies they are learning to numerous textbook paragraphs and longer passages from a wide range of academic disciplines. Students continue to learn new vocabulary in many activities, practice identifying main ideas and supporting details, use outlines and concept maps to make sure they understand the reading selections, and practice their inference skills in the contexts of excerpts taken primarily from current college textbooks.

Each activity in the Lab Manual is carefully constructed to ensure that students understand the purpose of the activity and can complete it successfully. The practice exercises begin with a succinct statement of the objective.

The Lab Manual also includes a skills awareness inventory sheet for each of the tutorial tests that students may take before they begin the course as well as achievement tests to discover how much they have learned by the end of the course. Three pairs of tests are available for students using *The Master Reader*: One is specifically designed for students in Florida who must pass the CLAST, a second is for Texas students who need to take the THEA, and a third is intended for more general use. The answer sheets are available in the back of the Lab Manual as well as report forms that foster metacognition. These report forms can be used as a portfolio activity to help assess student learning and growth.

For Instructors:

The Lab Manual is a collection of 78 activities designed to provide additional practice and enrichment for the skills in *The Master Reader*. Each chapter consists of five lab activities that can be used to add flexibility and interest to the classroom or for additional practice and for assessment purposes.

These lab activities provide students with a range of opportunities to practice becoming effective readers. The chapters of *The Master Reader* include numerous practices, applications, review tests, and mastery tests. The Lab Manual offers two practice exercises, two review tests, and two mastery tests that mirror the design of the text and emphasize the reading skills and applications students need to succeed in college. Students apply the strategies they are learning to numerous textbook paragraphs and longer passages from a wide range of academic disciplines.

Each activity in the Lab Manual is carefully constructed to ensure that students understand the purpose of the activity and can complete it successfully. The practice exercises begin with a succinct statement of the objective. The answer key to the manual is at the accompanying online site and is protected by instructor password. A report form is available at the end of the manual for students to keep a record of their scores and to track their progress.

The Lab Manual also includes a skills awareness inventory sheet for each of the tutorial tests that students may take before they begin the course as well as achievement tests to discover how much they have learned by the end of the course. Three pairs of tests are available for students using *The Master Reader*: One is specifically designed for students in Florida who must pass the CLAST, a second is for Texas students who need to take the THEA, and a third is intended for more general use. The answer sheets are available in the back of the Lab Manual as well as report forms that foster metacognition. These report forms can be used as a portfolio activity to help assess student learning and growth. The tutorial tests appear in the Instructor's Manual that accompanies *The Master Reader*, or you can access the tutorial tests by going to http://www.ablongman.com/henry and selecting *The Master Reader*.

The Effective Reader, 3e (available in November, 2010)
The Skilled Reader, 3e (available in November, 2010)
The Master Reader, 3e (available in December, 2010)

The series of skills-based textbooks, written by D. J. Henry of Daytona Beach Community College, features plentiful opportunities for students to practice individual and combined reading skills on high-interest passages from both textbooks and popular sources. Basic reading comprehension and vocabulary skills are addressed, and critical reading skills are introduced in careful step-by-step fashion.

The Henry series focuses students' attention on how their skills apply to reading college textbooks. The books also emphasize the importance of visuals, in addition to text, as valuable sources of information. Students are asked to respond to visuals throughout the series in Visual Vocabulary features. The Lab Manual offers 78 activities designed to provide additional practice and enrichment for all the topics in each book.

ABOUT THE LAB MANUAL AUTHOR

This manual is based upon much of the work of Susan Pongratz, who graduated from The College of William and Mary with a B.A. in English and an M.A. in Education. In addition to teaching developmental reading classes at Thomas Nelson Community College and co-coordinating the Verizon Reading Center there, she supervised student teachers for several years at Christopher Newport University. Since completing the Eastern Virginia Writing Project in 2002, she now serves as a teaching consultant, strongly espousing the philosophy of the reading/writing connection.

Mary Dubbé, who authored the revision of this Lab Manual, also teaches reading classes at Thomas Nelson Community College. She graduated from West Virginia University with an M.S. degree in language arts and an M.A. in reading. She has over 25 years of experience in preparing college students to be skilled readers and successful students. In addition to teaching, Mary is the director of learning communities on her campus, has presented workshops at several state and national conferences, and is a past the president of the Virginia Association of Developmental Education.

Name_____ Section _____ Date _____ Score (number correct) _____ x 10 = _____

Objective: To use the SQ3R reading method as an effective reading system.

Directions: Read the passage and answer the questions that follow.

1 In Shakespeare's *Julius Caesar*, Marc Antony, in giving the funeral oration for Caesar, says: "I come to bury Caesar, not to praise him. / The evil that men do lives after them; / The good is oft interred with their bones." And later: "For Brutus is an honourable man; / So are they all, all honourable men." But Antony, as we know, did come to praise Caesar and to convince the crowd that Brutus was not an honorable man.

2 In most messages there's an obvious meaning that you can derive from a literal reading of the words and sentences. But there's often another level of meaning; sometimes, as in *Julius Caesar*, it's the opposite of the literal meaning. At other times it seems totally unrelated. In reality, most messages have more than one level of meaning. Consider some frequently heard messages. Carol asks you how you like her new haircut. On one level, the meaning is clear: Do you like the haircut? But there's also another, perhaps more important, level: Carol is asking you to say something positive about her appearance. In the same way, the parent who complains about working hard at the office or in the home may, on a deeper level, be asking for an expression of appreciation. The child who talks about the unfairness of the other children in the playground may be asking for comfort and love. To appreciate these other messages you need to engage in depth listening.

3 If you respond only to the surface-level communication (the literal meaning), you miss the opportunity to make meaningful contact with the other person's feelings and needs. If you say to the parent, "You're always complaining. I bet you really love working so hard," you fail to respond to this call for understanding and appreciation. In regulating your surface and depth listening, consider the following guidelines:

- *Focus on both verbal and nonverbal messages.* Recognize both consistent and inconsistent "packages" of messages and use these as guides for drawing inferences about the speaker's meaning. Ask questions when in doubt. Listen also to what is omitted. Remember that speakers communicate by what they leave out as well as by what they include.

- *Listen for both content and relational messages.* The student who constantly challenges the teacher is, on one level, communicating disagreement over content. However, on another level—the relationship level—the student may be voicing objections to the instructor's authority or authoritarianism. The instructor needs to listen and respond to both types of messages.

- *Make special note of statements that refer to the speaker.* Remember that people inevitably talk about themselves. Whatever a person says is, in part, a function of who that person is. Attend carefully to those personal, self-reference messages.

- *Don't disregard the literal meaning of interpersonal messages in trying to uncover the hidden meaning.* Balance your listening between the surface and the underlying meaning. Respond to the different levels of meaning in the messages of others, as you would like others to respond to yours—be sensitive but not obsessive. Be attentive but not too eager to uncover hidden messages.

—Adapted from DeVito, *The Interpersonal Communication Book,* 11th ed., pp. 111–12.

1

_____ 1. All of the following would be helpful prior information in comprehending this passage *except*
_____.
   a. Julius Caesar was killed by Brutus and his fellow senators
   b. Communication can often be deceptive because there may be hidden messages within the text
   c. Mark Antony later became the ruler of Rome
   d. The word *literal* means *exact* or *word for word*

_____ 2. While surveying this passage, the master reader would first notice _____.
   a. the advice for instructors
   b. the bulleted information and the italicized words
   c. the irregular spelling of the word *honourable*
   d. the cautionary advice concerning meaningful communication

_____ 3. The master reader can conclude that the bulleted information _____.
   a. contains supplemental information that is probably not necessary in order to understand this article
   b. discloses historical facts about the background of Marc Antony's speech
   c. offers guidelines to help the reader listen more effectively
   d. lists the stages of communication

_____ 4. All of the following questions will help the master reader focus on the main ideas of the article *except* _____.
   a. Why did Brutus betray Julius Caesar?
   b. What is the difference between surface and depth listening?
   c. How do people communicate nonverbally?
   d. What is a relational message?

_____ 5. After surveying this passage, the reader can determine that the topic is _____.
   a. the great rulers of Rome
   b. Brutus, the friend who betrayed Caesar
   c. the aspects of surface listening and depth listening
   d. Shakespeare's play, *Julius Caesar*

_____ 6. The phrase *surface-level communication* in paragraph 3 most likely means _____.
   a. paying attention to the non-verbal messages of a speaker
   b. responding more to a speaker's emotions and feelings
   c. attending to relational messages
   d. listening to the exact words of the speaker and ignoring any underlying meaning

2

_____ 7. According to the information in paragraph 2, *depth listening* _____.
  a. is a very shallow means of communication
  b. will often reveal a different level of meaning
  c. is an extremely difficult communication skill
  d. is unimportant for most communication

_____ 8. The word *inferences* in the first bulleted item probably _____.
  a. refers to verbal messages
  b. refers to nonverbal messages
  c. refers to surface listening
  d. refers to explicitly stated messages

_____ 9. Since this passage suggests that listeners pay careful attention but not be too obsessive about finding hidden messages, the reader can conclude that _____.
  a. most people jump to wrong conclusions
  b. people usually disregard the literal meaning of interpersonal messages
  c. listeners can sometimes make wrong assumptions about what they hear
  d. most listeners have a built-in bias when it comes to interpersonal relationships

_____ 10. The purpose of this article is to _____.
  a. entertain the reader using the play, *Julius Caesar*
  b. inform the reader about the history of Rome
  c. persuade the reader of the importance of reading classical literature
  d. inform the reader about the need to engage in depth listening

Name_____ Section _____ Date _____ Score (number correct) _____ x 10 = _____

Objective: To use the SQ3R reading method as an effective reading system.

Directions: Read this selection from a college history textbook, then answer the questions that follow.

Eunice Williams/Gannenstenhawi

1 The sound of glass shattering and wood splintering woke seven-year-old Eunice Williams. Indians were ransacking the house. Her father shouted for help. Then footsteps pounded up the stairs and strangers rushed into her room. Strong hands yanked her out of bed and pushed her toward the stairs and down. John, only six, clung to her. The barn was ablaze. Her father, arms tied, was in his nightshirt. Indians taunted him with strange words and waved their hatchets before his face. After a time, several grabbed John and the baby and took them outside; another Indian followed with a club. Eunice's mother screamed but they held her back. After a few moments the Indians came back in and seized Parthena, a slave. They dragged her outside and her screams stopped.

2 Soon, morning light filtered through the broken window. The Indians untied one of Eunice's father's arms, gave him his pants and gestured for him to dress. They also thrust clothes toward her, and she put them on. Then she and her family were herded outside, where Parthena and Little John lay dead in the snow, and the baby in a heap near a boulder. The Indians rushed them into the meeting house. Inside, many of Eunice's neighbors were huddled against a wall. The Indians gave them all moccasins, and forced them to run toward the woods. Gunshots clattered at the far edge of the village, and the Indians made them run faster, deep into the forest. Those who lingered were dispatched with clubs or hatchets.

3 Throughout the day the captives scrambled onward. When Eunice stumbled and fell, exhausted, an Indian carried her on his shoulders, mile after mile. At night he covered her with a blanket. Sunrise brought the same frantic rush to the north. Eunice's mother, weakened from the new baby, fell behind. Her father tried to help her but could not. He paused with her to pray, but the Indians pushed him forward. Eunice never saw her mother again.

4 The Indians broke into smaller groups, and Eunice was separated from her father and brothers. The same Indian as before carried her. When they rested, he gave her the best pieces of meat. He smiled, saying something she didn't understand.

5 During the weeks that followed she was taken several hundred miles to a large Mohawk settlement near Montreal. There, the captive men were stripped naked and forced to run past the villagers, who beat and poked them with clubs and burning sticks. The women and children were treated more leniently. Their hair was cut; some had their ears pierced. Amidst great ceremony, they were immersed in water and their bodies were painted. Then they were given Mohawk clothing. Women wore loose sleeveless tunics, skirts that hung to their knees, leggings ornamented with moosehair, and leather moccasins. Their hair was greased and pulled back, fastened with a ribbon of eelskin.

6 Eunice was settled among a Mohawk family, and she came to understand that she had been adopted by them. But the family was unlike the one she had known. Mohawk husbands and wives lived apart from each other, with their own parents; children stayed with their mother and her large group of relatives.

7 In 1706, two years after Eunice had been taken from Deerfield, her father, a Puritan minister, was ransomed and returned home. Her older brothers were similarly "redeemed" soon afterward. But the Mohawks made no offer to redeem Eunice. In response to written pleas from her father, the Mohawks stated that they "would as soon part with their hearts" as with Eunice; besides, they added, the girl was "unwilling to return" to Massachusetts. In 1713 her father received word that his daughter had married a Mohawk.

—Adapted from Carnes and Garraty, *The American Nation,* 11th ed., pp. 92–93.

_____ 1. When skimming the title and first paragraph, a master reader would ask all of the following *except* _____.
    a. What does the word *ransacking* mean?
    b. What happened to Parthena?
    c. What do I already know about Native American Indians?
    d. What do I already know about the American Revolution?

_____ 2. A question which the master reader would formulate while skimming the entire passage would include all of the following *except* _____.
    a. Is this passage factual?
    b. Why did the Indians kidnap Eunice and her family?
    c. Why did the Indians kill some of the family, but not all?
    d. How were the Indians treated during the American Revolutionary War?

_____ 3. Which sentence would the active learner probably highlight as a main idea?
    a. Eunice was settled among a Mohawk family, and she came to understand that she had been adopted by them.
    b. Soon, morning light filtered through the broken window.
    c. At night he covered her with a blanket.
    d. He paused with her to pray, but the Indians pushed him forward.

_____ 4. According to the context, the best definition of *dispatch* is _____.
    a. transmitted
    b. sent
    c. posted
    d. killed

_____ 5. According to the context, the best definition of *redeemed* is _____?
    a. married
    b. tortured
    c. rescued
    d. lost

_____ 6. From this article, the master reader could assume that _____.
    a. Eunice's mother was able to escape
    b. Eunice's older brothers were ransomed and returned home.
    c. The Indians always treated their captives harshly
    d. Eunice's father did not do enough to help her

____ 7. The master reader could also conclude that _____.
   a. Eunice's father did not love her
   b. the Indians were waiting to ransom Eunice
   c. Eunice was much loved by her adopted family
   d. Eunice probably did not live long after her capture by the Indians

____ 8. This passage is organized according to _____.
   a. the sequence of events
   b. comparisons and contrasts of how the captives were treated
   c. causes and effects of Indian brutality
   d. reasons for mistreatment of captives

____ 9. This passage demonstrates that _____.
   a. Indians were unfairly represented in history books
   b. Indians were capable of both violence and kindness, much like most other societies
   c. Americans should never have settled in America
   d. Indians were unfairly treated by Americans

____ 10. Which sentence best summarizes this article?
   a. History is comprised of fictitious stories that represent what may have happened.
   b. Events of people's lives have no place in history books.
   c. American Indians were forced to turn to violent acts by the injustices imposed upon them by the American settlers.
   d. Although Eunice Williams was torn from her home and family, she learned to adjust to and eventually love the Mohawk family who adopted her.

Name_____ Section _____ Date _____ Score (number correct) _____ x 10 = _____

A. Directions: Use the reading system you have learned to answer the questions that follow these pages.

Gardner's Multiple Intelligences and Emotional Intelligence

1 Howard Gardner has proposed a theory that expands the definition of intelligence beyond those skills covered on an IQ test. Gardner identifies numerous intelligences that cover a range of human experience. The value of any of the abilities differs across human societies, according to what is needed by, useful to, and prized by a given society. As shown in Table 9.4, Gardner identified eight intelligences.

2 Gardner argues that Western society promotes the first two intelligences, whereas non-Western societies often value others. For example, in the Caroline Island of Micronesia, sailors must be able to navigate long distances without maps, using only their spatial intelligence and bodily kinesthetic intelligence. Such abilities count more in that society than the ability to write a term paper. In Bali, where artistic performance is part of everyday life, musical intelligence and talents involved in coordinating intricate dance steps are highly valued. Interpersonal intelligence is more central to collectivist societies such as Japan, where cooperative action and communal life are emphasized, than it is in individualistic societies such as the United States (Triandis, 1990).

3 Assessing these kinds of intelligence demands more than paper-and pencil tests and simple quantified measures. Gardner's theory of intelligence requires that the individual be observed and assessed in a variety of life situations as well as in the small slices of life depicted in traditional intelligence tests.

—Adapted from Gerrig and Zimbardo, *Psychology and Life*, 18th ed., p. 285.

_B_ 1. What is the topic of this selection?
   a. Gardner
   b. intelligence
   c. Gardner's multiple intelligences
   d. multiple personalities

_D_ 2. The central idea of this selection is _____.
   a. Gardner contends that people have multiple intelligences-abilities to solve a problem or create a product within a specific cultural setting
   b. Gardner contends that traditional intelligence tests do a good job of measuring a person's talent or ability within the framework of a specific cultural setting
   c. Intelligence testing is an easy and straightforward process
   d. Different societies promote different kinds of intelligence

7

___C___ 3. Which sentence would a psychology student most likely highlight in paragraph 1?
   a. Howard Gardner has proposed a theory that expands the definition of intelligence beyond those skills covered on an IQ test.
   b. Gardner identifies numerous intelligences that cover a range of human experience.
   c. The value of any of the abilities differs across human societies, according to what is needed by, useful to, and prized by a given society.
   d. As shown in Table 9.4, Gardner identified eight intelligences.

___A___ 4. The predominant pattern of paragraph 2 is _____.
   a. comparison and contrast because it presents pro and con views of Gardner's theory
   b. cause and effect because it presents the results of Gardner's test
   c. listing of details because it catalogs features of Gardner's intelligences
   d. listing of example because it provides examples of Gardner's types of intelligences

___B___ 5. "Assessing these kinds of intelligence demands more than paper-and pencil tests and simple quantified measures."

   From this sentence in the last paragraph, the reader can assume that _____.
   a. assessing Gardner's intelligences requires simple quantified measures
   b. Gardner does not support paper and pencil tests to measure intelligence
   c. Gardner's theory of intelligence has been adopted by most schools around the country
   d. assessing intelligence accurately is nearly impossible

B. Directions: Study the table below and answer the questions that follow it.

Table 9.4 Gardner's Eight Intelligences

Intelligence	End States	Core Components
Logical-mathematical	Scientist Mathematician	Sensitivity to, and capacity to discern, logical or numerical patterns; ability to handle long chains of reasoning
Linguistic	Poet Journalist	Sensitivity to the sounds, rhythms, and meanings of words; sensitivity to the different functions of language.
Naturalist	Biologist Environmentalist	Sensitivity to the differences among diverse species; abilities to interact subtly with living creatures.
Musical	Composer Violinist	Abilities to produce and appreciate rhythm, pitch, and timbre; appreciation of the forms of musical expressiveness.
Spatial	Navigator Sculptor	Capacities to perceive the visual-spatial world accurately and to perform transformations on one's initial perceptions.
Bodily kinesthetic	Dancer Athlete	Abilities to control one's body movements and to handle objects skillfully.
Interpersonal	Therapist Salesperson	Capacities to discern and respond appropriately to the moods, temperaments, motivations, and desires of other people.
Intrapersonal	Person with detailed, accurate self-knowledge	Access to one's own feelings and the ability to discriminate among them and draw upon them to guide behavior, knowledge of one's own strengths, weaknesses, desires, and intelligences.

—Gerrig and Zimbardo, *Psychology and Life,* 18th ed., p. 286.

_C_ 6. In the table, the heading "End States" refers to _____.
   a. a learning style
   b. a typical example or model
   c. a sample of intelligence
   d. a quality of a learning style

_A_ 7. From the table, the master reader could infer that a person should _____.
   a. consider his or her personal preferences when deciding a career path
   b. select the most lucrative career path regardless of current trends
   c. select the career that is most in demand regardless of personal preferences
   d. try to develop additional types of intelligences in order to be more productive

_C_ 8. From the table, the reader could infer that there is a similarity in intelligences between _____.
   a. chefs and dancers because they both require movement
   b. navigators and gymnasts because they both require learning sequences
   c. poets and journalists because they both work with words
   d. mathematicians and musicians because they use logical steps

_B_ 9. From the table, the reader could infer that people with an interpersonal intelligence _____.
   a. are very introspective and keep to themselves and their own thoughts
   b. focus on the inner thoughts of others, the reasons for their actions, and ways to change their responses
   c. avoid contact with other people; instead, they choose to remain alone
   d. should avoid careers that require them to mediate conflicts or negotiate contracts

_B_ 10. From the table, the reader could infer that people with an intrapersonal intelligence _____.
   a. are more introspective and have a realistic and accurate understanding about themselves
   b. focus intently on the thoughts and feelings of others
   c. often have deep psychological problems that require extensive therapy
   d. need others to point out their talents and to give them direction

Chapter 1: A Reading System for Master Readers
LAB 1.4 REVIEW TEST 2

Name_____ Section _____ Date _____ Score (number correct) _____ x 10 = _____

Objective: To use the SQ3R reading method as an effective reading system.

Directions: Read the passage and answer the questions that follow.

Auto Insurance Policy Provisions

[1]Auto insurance insures against damage to an automobile and expenses associated with accidents. [2]In this way, it protects one of your main assets (your car) and also limits your potential liabilities (expenses due to an accident). [3]If you own or drive a car, you need auto insurance. [4]Policies are purchased for a year or six months at property and casualty insurance companies. [5]Your policy specifies the amount of coverage if you are legally liable for bodily injury, if you and your passengers incur medical bills, and if your car is damaged as the result of an accident or some other event (such as a tree falling on the car).

[6]An **insurance policy** is a contract between the insurance company and the policy holder. [7]An **auto insurance policy** specifies the coverage (including dollar limits) provided by an insurance company for a particular individual and vehicle. [8]The contract identifies the policy holder and family members who are also insured if they use the insured vehicle. [9]You should have insurance information such as your policy number and the name of a contact person at the insurance company with you when you drive. [10]If you are in an accident, exchange your insurance information with that of the other driver and also fill out a police report.

—Adapted from Madura, *Personal Finance*, 2nd ed., p. 295.

1. All of the following would be helpful prior information in comprehending this passage *except*
    _____.
    a. information about different types of car insurance
    b. information about problems with car insurance
    c. information providing a list of all insurance companies
    d. information about the different types of coverage offered by car insurance

2. While surveying this passage, the master reader will first notice _____.
    a. the time limits for car insurance policies
    b. the title and the bold-face words
    c. the kinds of coverage provided by car insurance
    d. the information needed if in an accident

3. Why are the two phrases in the second paragraph in boldface print?
    a. These phrases form a natural separation between the paragraphs.
    b. These words are the only important words in the passage.
    c. These are important terms defined in the passage that the reader should study.
    d. The words in boldface print are not significant to the understanding of this passage.

10

A 4. Which of the following questions will help the effective reader focus on the main ideas of the article?

    a. What provisions are provided by an auto insurance policy?
    b. What is the difference between auto insurance and home-owners insurance?
    c. How do people purchase an auto insurance police?
    d. What is a contract?

C 5. After surveying this passage, the reader can determine that the topic is _____.

    a. the most reliable auto insurance companies
    b. auto insurance providers
    c. auto insurance policies
    d. policy holders

A 6. The word *assets* in paragraph 1 most likely means _____.

    a. favorable traits
    b. useful items
    c. benefit
    d. property of value

B 7. According to the information in paragraph 1, *potential liabilities* are _____.

    a. not very common
    b. possible expenses due to an accident
    c. the result of a good driving record
    d. the costs associated with auto insurance

B 8. The phrase *legally liable* in the first paragraph probably refers to _____.

    a. damages for which you are not responsible
    b. responsibility according to the law
    c. justification for aggressive driving
    d. protection against uninsured drivers

C 9. Since this passage states that family members can also be included in a car insurance policy, the reader can conclude that _____.

    a. family members will not be held responsible if they cause an accident
    b. family members will not be covered if they are injured in an accident
    c. family members in the policy will be covered in case of an accident
    d. family members will not be covered in case of an accident

D 10. The purpose of this article is to _____.

    a. entertain the reader using examples of humorous insurance stories
    b. inform the reader about the problems associated with car insurance
    c. persuade the reader of the importance to purchase car insurance form reputable companies
    d. inform the reader about automobile insurance

Name_____ Section _____ Date _____ Score (number correct) _____ x 10 = _____

Directions: Read the following selection from a college humanities textbook and answer the questions that follow:

1 Leonardo goes far beyond surface realism in the masterpiece, the *Mona Lisa* of 1503-1505. The work has become the most famous single work of art in the world, still attracting huge numbers of visitors each day to the Louvre Museum in Paris.

2 What is all the fuss about? How do we account for the extraordinary stature of this relatively small canvas in the world of humanities? One reason, of course, may be that widely discussed mysterious smile. One does not find many smiles in portrait paintings, because the artist has customarily been hired to render both a realistic likeness and an idealization in the classic mode. Her famous, and still mysterious, smile particularizes Mona Lisa Giaconda, whom Leonardo was commissioned to paint. She is not only idealized in the traditional manner of portraiture, but she is also an individual woman captured in a particular inner action at a particular time.

3 A closer look at the painting, however, reveals that the mouth is shown with only the faintest trace of a smile. Just as interesting is that Signora Giaconda is looking at something not shown in the painting—just what we can never know—which adds to the mystery. (Hint: If you'd like to leave behind a painting or a poem that people will still be talking about centuries from now, be sure there is an unsolvable mystery about it.)

4 The following experiment, suggested by one art critic, can be performed right at this moment. Cover the left side of the face, using your hand or an index card. Presumably, you will see a warm, sensuous woman, gazing provocatively—at you! Now cover the right side, and presumably you will see an aristocrat who finds something (not you, of course) mildly amusing. Many have said that Leonardo in this work has revealed the essential ambiguity of all human faces and personalities. If we agree, then we could say that the *Mona Lisa* accomplishes a goal many artists seek but rarely achieve: Its creator has both particularized and generalized his subject. What should, however, stand out in our mind is that the portrait is a supreme example of the Renaissance movement toward individualism or, an organic part of the rebellion against the medieval emphasis on an afterlife rather than on the rich diversity of this life.

5 Some one hundred years later, Shakespeare created monumental and decidedly individual characters such as Hamlet, Othello, Lear, Macbeth, Lady Macbeth, and Cleopatra. Yes, they offer insights into many universal human traits and weaknesses, but they are also three-dimensional beings firmly rooted in their unique situations and speaking in a language so specific to each that lovers of Shakespeare can usually identify major characters even when all names are omitted from the text.

—Adapted from Janaro and Altshuler, *The Art of Being Human*, 8th ed., pp. 159–160.

_____ 1. What is the topic of this selection?
   a. the ambiguity of faces
   b. the most famous painting in the world, the *Mona Lisa*
   c. theories behind the mysterious smile of the *Mona Lisa*
   d. Shakespeare's memorable characters

_____ 2. All of the following questions will help the effective reader focus on the main ideas of this article *except* _____.
   a. Why is the *Mona Lisa* so famous?
   b. Where is the *Mona Lisa* housed?
   c. Why is the *Mona Lisa* such an important painting?
   d. Where was Leonardo da Vinci born?

_____ 3. Which of the following items would *not* be necessary prior information to understand paragraphs 1 and 2?
   a. what the *Mona Lisa* looks like
   b. the knowledge that the *Mona Lisa* is a portrait of a real person
   c. the knowledge of the name of the architect of the Louvre
   d. speculation about the mysteries surrounding the *Mona Lisa*

_____ 4. To better understand the passage, what prior information about the Renaissance would be helpful?
   a. The word *renaissance* means "rebirth."
   b. Many of the Renaissance's works were devoted to religious themes.
   c. Prior to the Renaissance, Medieval art stressed the afterlife, but Renaissance art focused on leading a good life in the present world.
   d. The center of renaissance art was in or around Florence, Italy, and the artists presented new ways of seeing life.

_____ 5. "Presumably, you will see a warm, sensuous woman, gazing provocatively—at you!"

   The word *provocatively* most likely means _____.
   a. in a serious manner
   b. in a sad and gloomy manner
   c. in an enticing and teasing manner
   d. in an anxious and fearful manner

_____ 6. To better understand the results of the experiment suggested by the art critic, a reader can surmise that an aristocrat was _____.
   a. a peasant who works for a landowner
   b. a wealthy person with family connections and land holdings
   c. a painter who traveled the countryside seeking mysterious subjects
   d. a sculptor who emphasized realism

___ 7. "What should, however, stand out in our mind is that the portrait is a supreme example of the Renaissance movement toward individualism or, an organic part of the rebellion against the medieval emphasis on an afterlife rather than in the rich diversity of this life."

The word *diversity* most likely means _____.
a. variety
b. commonplace
c. ordinary
d. heavenly

___ 8. "Some one hundred years later, Shakespeare created monumental and decidedly individual characters like Hamlet, Othello, Lear, Macbeth, Lady Macbeth, and Cleopatra."

The word *monumental* most likely means _____.
a. suitable for praise
b. cast in marble
c. small symbols
d. unrecognizable

___ 9. "Yes, they offer insights into many universal human traits and weaknesses, but they are also three-dimensional beings firmly rooted in their unique situations and speaking in a language so specific to each that lovers of Shakespeare can usually identify major characters even when all names are omitted from the text."

The word *three-dimensional* implies that the characters are _____.
a. only a dot on the page
b. flat drawings by the playwright
c. dynamic characters with good and bad attributes
d. shadows of the real people they represent

___ 10. Paragraph 5 implies that _____.
a. Shakespeare, like Renaissance painters and sculptors, aimed for realism and idealization in his characters
b. Shakespeare should have taken note of the works of da Vinci
c. Shakespeare should have used Florence, Italy, as a setting for all of his plays
d. Shakespeare was heavily influenced by the medieval period

Name_____ Section _____ Date _____ Score (number correct) _____ x 10 = _____

Directions: Read the complete nutrition section and answer the questions that follow.

Nutrigenomics

1 Nutrigenomics is a scientific discipline studying the interactions between genes, the environment, and nutrition. For decades, the conventional wisdom has been that the genes a person is born with determine that person's fate. But the theory behind nutrigenomics is that our genes might not matter as much as what we eat or that to which we expose our body.

Gene Alteration

2 Scientists have known for some time that diet and environmental factors can contribute to disease, but what has not been understood before is how these factors contribute to disease by altering how our genes are expressed. Nutrigenomics proposes that foods and environmental factors can act like a switch in body cells, turning on some genes while turning off others. When a gene is activated, it will instruct the cell to create a protein that will show up as a physical characteristic or functional ability, such as a pigment that makes the agouti's fur yellow, or a protein that facilitates the storage of fat. When a gene is switched off, the cell will not create that protein, and the organism's form or function will differ. Factors thought most likely to affect gene activation include smoking, drug and alcohol use, exposure to carcinogens, radiation, stress, physical activity level, socioeconomic status, and particularly nutrition, since our genes are continually exposed to the components of our diet.

Effects on Our Children

3 In addition, nutrigenomics scientists are discovering that what we eat or that to which we expose our genes—food, smoke, etc.—can affect gene expression not only in the exposed organism, but also in his or her offspring. In short, nutrigenomics proposes that foods and environmental factors can influence not only our own genes, but also the genes of our children. It's an intriguing theory—but is there any real evidence to support it?

> —Adapted from Thompson and Manore, *Nutrition: An Applied Approach,* 2nd ed., pp. 33–34.

_____ 1. What is the topic of this passage?
   a. dieting
   b. nutrigenomics
   c. scientific theories
   d. gene alteration

_____ 2. After surveying the title, headings, and first paragraph, what will most likely follow?
   a. reasons people diet
   b. the scientists who study nutrigenomics
   c. an explanation of the possible effects of nutrigenomics on our genes
   d. a comparison of American diets past and present

_____ 3. Questions which a student might form after surveying and before reading this passage would include all of the following *except*
   a. What is nutrigenomics?
   b. What are the effects of nutrigenomics on our genes?
   c. How will nutrigenomics affect our children?
   d. What other environmental issues affect our health?

_____ 4. According to the context of paragraph 1, nutrigenomics involves interactions among all of the following *except* _____.
   a. economics
   b. genes
   c. environment
   d. nutrition

_____ 5. According to the context of paragraph 2, *gene expression* means _____.
   a. having more than one gene
   b. using a gene to make a protein that affects the body's form or function
   c. using radiation to change the nature of our genes
   d. tracing all the genes in our body

_____ 6. According to the context of paragraph 2, *socioeconomic status* mostly likely refers to_____.
   a. an individual's influence in a community
   b. one's race or religion
   c. the classification of an individual according to social and economic factors
   d. the employment factors associated with one's level of education

_____ 7. According to this passage, what we are exposed to _____.
   a. will have no effect on our children
   b. can guarantee beneficial changes in our children
   c. will increase the likelihood of birth defects in our children
   d. can help or harm our children

_____ 8. Based on the information in paragraph 3, nutrigenomics _____.
   a. is a theory that will need supporting evidence
   b. is a proven fact
   c. is agreed upon by all scientists
   d. is viewed as a fraudulent theory by most scientists

16

_____ 9. Which sentence in paragraph 3 should a master reader highlight?
   a. In addition, nutrigenomics scientists are discovering that what we expose our genes to—food, smoke, etc.—can affect gene expression not only in the exposed organism, but also in his or her offspring.
   b. In short, nutrigenomics proposes that foods and environmental factors can influence not only our own genes, but also the genes of our children.
   c. It's an intriguing theory—but is there any real evidence to support it?
   d. None of these sentences is important.

_____ 10. Which one of the following sentences best summarizes this article?
   a. Nutrigenomics is a relatively new science.
   b. Scientists around the world are beginning to study nutrigenomics.
   c. Some scientists support the theory of nutrigenomics which proposes that exposure to certain foods and environmental factors can have positive or negative affects on the genes in our bodies.
   d. The concept of gene alteration is a new development that needs much research and study before it is put into practice.

Chapter 2: Vocabulary Skills
LAB 2.1 PRACTICE EXERCISE 1

Name_____ Section _____ Date _____ Score (number correct) _____ x 10 = _____

Objective: To determine the definitions of unfamiliar words by using context clues.

Directions: Using the context clues and your knowledge of word parts, select the best definition for the word in **bold** print.

_____ 1. Marcel can throw together a well-organized **impromptu** speech on nearly any topic he is given.
   a. planned
   b. prepared
   c. spontaneous
   d. arranged

_____ 2. Although the no-smoking sign was prominently displayed, the tour guide **reiterated** the no-smoking policy by saying in a firm voice, "Smoking is forbidden in this area."
   a. repeated
   b. wrote
   c. drew
   d. withdrew

_____ 3. Gordon nervously clutched the engagement ring and **vacillated** between wanting to spend the rest of his life with Latisha and extending the freedom of bachelorhood a few more years.
   a. frequented
   b. married
   c. commanded
   d. wavered

_____ 4. Before the Civil War, South Carolina was the first Southern state to **secede** from the Union. By February 1861, six other states had also separated themselves and sent representatives to a meeting to form the Confederate States of America.
   a. join
   b. withdraw
   c. fight
   d. train

_____ 5. Despite the less interesting scenery, Damon prefers to drive on the straight highways of the interstate and bypass the **sinuous** roadways that were built to follow rivers and mountain paths.
   a. easy
   b. dark
   c. winding
   d. strange

Directions: Using the information in the chart and the context of each sentence, select the word that best fits the meaning of the sentence. Use each word once.

Prefix	Meaning	Root	Meaning	Suffix	Meaning
mono-	one	*lith*	stone	*-ic*	of, like, relate to, being
				-ous	
neo-	new	*gamos*	marriage	*-graphy*	writing
		logos	speak		

____ 6. Invented in the late 1700s, _____ is a form of printing from a flat metal or plastic plate or stone.

        a. monolith
        b. monologues
        c. Neolithic
        d. lithography
        e. monogamous

____ 7. Traditional marriages in the Western world during the twentieth century were expected to be life-long and _____.
        a. monolith
        b. monologues
        c. Neolithic
        d. lithography
        e. monogamous

____ 8. The _____ Age marked an important stage in humankind's development. Humans solved many of the problems faced during the Old Stone Age and established villages, religion, art, architecture, farming, advanced tools, and weapons.
        a. monolith
        b. monologues
        c. Neolithic
        d. lithography
        e. monogamous

____ 9. Ayers Rock, the world's largest _____, is 2.2 miles long, 1.5 miles wide, and rises 348 meters above the flat, arid land of the Amadeus Basin in Australia.
        a. monolith
        b. monologues
        c. Neolithic
        d. lithography
        e. monogamous

____ 10. Melissa became a more effective parent when she replaced her angry _____ to her teenage son with listening skills that began an ongoing dialogue between them.
        a. monolith
        b. monologues
        c. Neolithic
        d. lithography
        e. monogamous

Chapter 2: Vocabulary Skills
LAB 2.2 PRACTICE EXERCISE 2

Name_____ Section _____ Date _____ Score (number correct) _____ x 10 = _____

Objective: To determine the definitions of unfamiliar words by using context clues.

Directions: Using the context clues and your knowledge of word parts, select the best definition for the word in **boldfaced** print.

_____ 1. Lisa's **sanguine** disposition charmed all who met her; in contrast, her roommate's consistently sad manner disgusted the people she encountered.
   a. gloomy
   b. angry
   c. cheerful
   d. moody

_____ 2. Because of the conflicts over Medicare revisions, a **brouhaha** developed in the Senate as Republicans and Democrats waged attacks and counterattacks on each other.
   a. silence
   b. uproar
   c. agreement
   d. cooperative spirit

_____ 3. The politician's mistake was so **egregious** that the entire community found it impossible to forgive him.
   a. unremarkable
   b. appreciative
   c. obviously bad
   d. adaptable

_____ 4. Unlike her brother who avoided making any noble gestures, Elizabeth **magnanimously** offered to provide a copy of her notes for each lecture.
   a. generously
   b. seriously
   c. reluctantly
   d. insistently

_____ 5. Andrew quickly discovered that listening to the abridged version of *The Crucible* could not **supplant** actually reading Arthur Miller's play, and he suddenly wished he had not tried to substitute an easy way out for hard work.
   a. examine
   b. improve
   c. suspect
   d. substitute

20

_____ 6. Although Emma **purports** to have compassion for everyone, what she claims is very different from what she does. She is quick to spread gossip, whether or not it is kind or even true.
    a. propels
    b. claims
    c. avoids
    d. investigates

_____ 7. The **vendetta** between the Capulets and the Montagues in *Romeo and Juliet* is one of the most famous feuds in literature.
    a. friendly gathering
    b. feud
    c. romance
    d. cultivation

_____ 8. With more than 50 novels and short stories written since 1974 when *Carrie* was published, Stephen King is one of the most **prolific** writers of modern American fiction.
    a. productive
    b. unpopular
    c. difficult to comprehend
    d. unknown

_____ 9. The director of the food bank faced a desk **replete** with requests from people in need following the hurricane disaster; however, there was a scarcity of donations and few prospects for more contributions.
    a. filled
    b. customary and usual
    c. unusual
    d. expensive

_____ 10. Our supervisor's disposition is **mercurial**; just when he seems calm and appreciative of our work, he begins to shout and complain about all of his employees who lack talent or devotion to the company.
    a. calm
    b. sensitive
    c. silently thoughtful
    d. quickly changeable

Chapter 2: Vocabulary Skills
LAB 2.3 REVIEW TEST 1

Name_____ Section _____ Date _____ Score (number correct) _____ x 10 = _____

A. Directions: Using the context clues and your knowledge of word parts, select the best definition for the word in **bold** print.

[1]Culture is **transmitted** from one generation to another through **enculturation,** a process by which you learn the culture into which you are born (your native culture). [2]A different process of learning culture is **acculturation,** the process by which you learn the rules and norms of a culture different from your native culture. [3]Through acculturation, your original or native culture is modified by direct contact with (or exposure to) a new and different culture

—Devito, *The Interpersonal Communication Book*, 10th ed., p. 37.

_____ 1. What is the best meaning of the word **transmitted** in sentence 1?
   a.   passed on
   b.   determined
   c.   localized
   d.   changed

_____ 2. What is the best meaning of the word **enculturation** in sentence 1?
   a.   the process of transforming oneself from one culture to another
   b.   the process of adapting to a new culture
   c.   the process by which you learn your native culture
   d.   the process of learning to let go of your native culture

_____ 3. What is the best meaning of the word **acculturation** in sentence 2?
   a.   the process of clinging to one's culture in spite of exposure to another
   b.   the process by which your culture is changed through contract with another culture
   c.   the process by which you learn your native culture
   d.   the process of learning to let go of your native culture

[1]Relationships may be viewed on a **continuum,** from the impersonal at one end to highly personal (that is, interpersonal) at the other end. [2]**Interpersonal** relationships are those that exist between people who are interdependent, where one person's behavior has a significant impact on the other person. [3]We can distinguish interpersonal relationships from **impersonal** relationships on the basis of three main factors: psychological data, explanatory knowledge, and personally established rules.

— DeVito, *The Interpersonal Communication Book*, 10th ed., p. 234.

_____ 4. What is the best meaning of the word **continuum** in sentence 1?
   a.   a range
   b.   a nonstop relationship
   c.   a continuing conflict
   d.   a close friend

_____ 5. What is the best meaning of the word **interpersonal** in sentence 2?
   a. between cultures
   b. between people
   c. characteristic of possessive relationship
   d. characteristic of a passive relationship

_____ 6. What is the best meaning of the word **impersonal** in sentence 3?
   a. highly personal
   b. not personal
   c. very friendly
   d. very unfriendly

[1]Touch communication, also referred to as **haptics**, is perhaps the most **primitive** form of communication. [2]**Developmentally**, touch is probably the first sense to be used; even in the womb, the child is stimulated by touch. [3]Soon after birth, the child is **fondled**, caressed, patted, and stroked. In turn, the child explores its world through touch. [4]In a very short time, the child learns to communicate a wide variety of meanings through touch.

— DeVito, *The Interpersonal Communication Book*, 10th ed., p. 189.

_____ 7. What is the best meaning of the word **haptics** in sentence 1?
   a. a form of happiness achieved through psychology
   b. touch communication
   c. developmental speech
   d. learning through listening

_____ 8. What is the best meaning of the word **primitive** in sentence 2?
   a. complicated and serious
   b. humorous and light
   c. earliest and basic
   d. interesting

_____ 9. What is the best meaning of the word **developmentally** in sentence 2?
   a. a process of renewing energy and strength
   b. a process of acquiring wealth
   c. a process of assessing health
   d. a process of growing and changing

_____ 10. What is the best meaning of the word **fondled** in sentence 3?
   a. stroked lovingly
   b. touched in an aggressive way
   c. handled with unconcern
   d. mauled with intent to harm

Chapter 2: Vocabulary Skills
LAB 2.4 REVIEW TEST 2

Name_____ Section _____ Date _____ Score (number correct) _____ x 10 = _____

Directions: Using the context clues and your knowledge of word parts, select the best definition for the word in **bold** print.

_____ 1. Heather and John want an **idyllic** wedding in the peaceful, simple beauty of the rose garden at Washington Oakes State Park.
  a. inexpensive
  b. expensive
  c. formal
  d. tranquil

_____ 2. A mental **aberration** such as paranoia (irrational fear) clouds reasonable thought.
  a. abnormality
  b. creativity
  c. test
  d. headache

_____ 3. Adolph Hitler sought to **eradicate**, or wipe out, the Jewish population as one of his primary missions.
  a. discharge
  b. exonerate
  c. destroy
  d. energize

_____ 4. Sniffing glue may seem like **innocuous** fun; however, inhaling dangerous chemical vapors can cause death by suffocation or heart failure.
  a. dangerous
  b. harmless
  c. severe
  d. indecent

_____ 5. Kobe Bryant was considered a sports **paragon** until allegations of rape threatened to ruin his reputation and turn him into a fallen hero.
  a. enthusiast
  b. addict
  c. expert
  d. shining example

Directions: Using the information in the chart and the context of each sentence, select the word that best fits the meaning of the sentence. Use each word once.

Prefix	Meaning	Root	Meaning	Suffix	Meaning
e-	out, from	*ferv*	hot, burning, glowing	*-ent*	of, like
				-or	one who does something
				-ment	act or state
				-tion	act or state

_____ 6. Mr. Gunshannon's _____ (passion) for literature makes his classes exciting.
    a. effervescent (adj.)
    b. fervent (adj.)
    c. fervor (n.)
    d. ferment (v.)
    e. fermentation (n.)

_____ 7. Unlike her bland and quiet sister, Margarita has a(n) _____ personality, and she extends an outward welcome to everyone.
    a. effervescent (adj.)
    b. fervent (adj.)
    c. fervor (n.)
    d. ferment (v.)
    e. fermentation (n.)

_____ 8. Highly successful professional athletes possess a _____ dedication to their sports.
    a. effervescent (adj.)
    b. fervent (adj.)
    c. fervor (n.)
    d. ferment (v.)
    e. fermentation (n.)

_____ 9. A skilled brewer carefully controls the _____ system to produce a beer of superior and consistent quality.
    a. effervescent (adj.)
    b. fervent (adj.)
    c. fervor (n.)
    d. ferment (v.)
    e. fermentation (n.)

_____ 10. The starter for sourdough bread must be allowed to _____ for about a week before you can use it in your recipes.
    a. effervescent (adj.)
    b. fervent (adj.)
    c. fervor (n.)
    d. ferment (v.)
    e. fermentation (n.)

Name_____ Section _____ Date _____ Score (number correct) _____ x 10 = _____

A. Directions: Using the context clues and your knowledge of word parts, select the best definition for the word in **boldfaced** print.

____ 1. For nearly 50 years, Jean Piaget developed **theories** about the ways that children think, reason, and solve problems.
   a. ideas
   b. facts
   c. products
   d. intelligence

____ 2. Jean Piaget gave the name **schemes** to the mental structures that help individuals understand the world.
   a. tricks
   b. visions
   c. frameworks
   d. opinions

____ 3. An infant's first schemes are based on **sensorimotor** systems such as sucking, looking, grasping, and pushing.
   a. emotional
   b. physical
   c. awkward
   d. skilled

____ 4. Instead of being filled with her usual patience and understanding, Shajuana was surprisingly **devoid** of sympathy for her boyfriend's excuses.
   a. empty
   b. full
   c. tired
   d. giving

____ 5. Although the no-smoking sign was prominently displayed, the tour guide **reiterated** the no-smoking policy by saying in a firm voice, "Smoking is forbidden in this area."
   a. summarized
   b. avoided
   c. repeated
   d. ignored

B. Directions: Read the following passage from a college social science textbook and use the context clues and your knowledge of word parts to determine the best meaning of the underlined words.

Society and Change

[1]For most of human history, people born in one generation lived very much like their parents and could count on their children living very much as they had. [2]Whatever change occurred was almost **imperceptible** because it was so slow. [3]For the past 250 years, and especially for the past 50 years, such vast changes have taken place from one generation to the next that people separated by 20 or 30 years may be said to live in an altogether different society and be strangers to one another. [4]**Futurologist** Alvin Toffler has called this concept "future shock," a condition akin to the culture shock that would be experienced by a person **confronting** a totally alien culture for the first time.

[5]At the same time that dramatic changes constantly take place, a thread of stability is also apparent. [6]The factor of stability holds societies together and **binds** each generation to the next.

[7]The subject of change holds special fascination for social scientists because, if the sources of change could be determined scientifically and the course of change predicted, then the possibility of guiding change in the direction of attaining the highest common good could become a reality. [8]Unfortunately, the subject of change is not so easily **harnessed**.

—Adapted from Perry and Perry, *Contemporary Society: An Introduction to Social Science*, 12th ed., p. 263.

_____ 6. What is the best meaning of the word **imperceptible** in sentence 2?
    a. obvious
    b. hardly noticeable
    c. clear
    d. destroyed

_____ 7. What is the best meaning of the word **futurologist** in sentence 4?
    a. an archeologist
    b. a fortune-teller
    c. one who studies extinct societies
    d. one who studies the future

_____ 8. What is the best meaning of the word **confronting** in sentence 4?
    a. facing
    b. avoiding
    c. describing
    d. leaving

_____ 9. What is the best meaning of the word **binds** in sentence 6?
    a. ties with rope
    b. unfastens
    c. connects
    d. forces

_____ 10. What is the best meaning of the word **harnessed** in sentence 9?
    a. let loose
    b. yoked together
    c. forgotten
    d. controlled

Name_____ Section _____ Date _____ Score (number correct) _____ x 10 = _____

A. Directions: Using the context clues and your knowledge of word parts, select the best definition for the word in **boldfaced** type.

_____ 1. Excellent students do not rely only on **extrinsic** goals such as grades; they also heavily rely on the intrinsic, or inner, motivation to learn.
   a. internal
   b. lofty
   c. outer
   d. concrete

_____ 2. Some believe that manufacturers create **factitious** demands for their products by spreading rumors of shortages when none exists.
   a. factual
   b. artificial
   c. expensive
   d. cheap

_____ 3. When the educational process comes to **fruition,** the accomplishment of getting that diploma is itself a great reward and makes the years of hard work worthwhile.
   a. bitterness
   b. joy
   c. frustration
   d. fulfillment

_____ 4. Grief is composed of several **transitory** stages that one must move through in order to fully recover from a great loss.
   a. permanent
   b. purposeful
   c. painful
   d. temporary

_____ 5. Instead of choosing light, heartening comedies or romances, Marlena prefers dark, **harrowing** movies such as *Seven* and the American version of the Japanese film *The Ring*.
   a. entertaining
   b. disturbing
   c. encouraging
   d. failing

B. Directions: Read the following passage from a college social-science textbook and use the context clues and your knowledge of word parts to determine the best meaning of the underlined words.

Is Milk Just for Babies?

[1]Infants thrive on an all-milk diet, but most adults cannot digest milk. [2]About 75% of people worldwide, including 25% of those in the United States, lose the ability to digest lactose, or "milk sugar," in early childhood, and they become lactose **intolerant**. [3]Roughly 75% of African Americans, Hispanics, and Native Americans, as well as 90% of Asian Americans, are lactose intolerant. [4]Only a relatively small proportion of people, primarily those of northern European descent, **retain** the ability to digest lactose into adulthood.

[5]Lactose intolerance arises when the body stops producing the enzyme lactase, which **catalyses** the breakdown of lactose. [6]When someone who lacks this enzyme consumes milk products, undigested lactose draws water in the intestines by osmosis and also feeds intestinal bacteria that produce gas. [7]The **surplus** of water and gas lead to abdominal pain, bloating, diarrhea, and flatulence—a rather high price to pay for indulging in ice cream. [8]But compared with the consequences of other enzyme deficiencies, the inability to tolerate milk is a relatively **negligible** inconvenience.

—Adapted from Audesirk, Audesirk, and Byers, *Life on Earth*, 5th ed., p. 79.

_____ 6. What is the best meaning of the word **intolerant** in sentence 2?
   a. narrow-minded
   b. prejudiced
   c. easily annoyed
   d. allergic

_____ 7. What is the best meaning of the word **retain** in sentence 4?
   a. maintain
   b. lose
   c. forget
   d. develop

_____ 8. What is the best meaning of the word **catalyses** in sentence 5?
   a. discourages
   b. prevents
   c. brings about
   d. eliminates

_____ 9. What is the best meaning of the word **surplus** in sentence 7?
   a. additional requirements
   b. excess
   c. extra money
   d. removal

_____ 10. What is the best meaning of the word **negligible** in sentence 8?
   a. significant
   b. important
   c. minor
   d. catastrophic

Chapter 3: Stated Main Ideas
LAB 3.1 PRACTICE EXERCISE 1

Name_____ Section _____ Date _____ Score (number correct) _____ x 10 = _____

Objective: To determine topics and main ideas.

Directions: Consider the following sets of ideas. Two are specific statements that support the general main idea statement. Select the statement that could serve as a topic sentence for the other two.

_____ 1. Which statement could serve as a main idea for the other two?

    a. One trend in economic globalization is to send many jobs to other countries such as India, Pakistan, and the Philippines.

    b. Today's students will need high-level training in math, writing, critical reading, and critical thinking to compete for the high-salary jobs that remain in the United States.

    c. Economic globalization has created new trends and dilemmas for the current workforce.

_____ 2. Which statement could serve as a main idea for the other two?

    a. Anagrams are words that are formed by reorganizing the letters of another such as altitude and latitude.

    b. Given opportunities to play with words, children can increase their vocabulary and improve their spelling.

    c. Think Pink is a game in which the participant gives two clue words and the other player must come up with rhyming synonyms: for example, a "seafood platter" might be a "fish dish."

_____ 3. Which statement could serve as a main idea for the other two?

    a. Cell phones, while convenient, have created some new problems.

    b. Motorists are literally being driven to distraction when they try to maneuver their vehicle and simultaneously negotiate a cell phone conversation.

    c. Administrators at one university discovered a cheating ring that involved cell phone use during exams, which led to the ban of phones in classes.

_____ 4. Which statement could serve as a main idea for the other two?

    a. Years ago, firefighters used unlit cigars as air filters when they entered a smoke-filled building.

    b. Today's firefighter wears turnout gear made of a fire-resistant material called Nomax and carries a self-contained breathing apparatus.

    c. The equipment created for today's firefighters helps keep them out of harm's way.

_____ 5. Which statement could serve as a main idea for the other two?

    a. Hamlet is an example of a dynamic, or multidimensional, character; that is, he evolves as he interacts with others in the play.

    b. In contrast, Laertes is a static, or monodimensional, character, who acts as a foil to Hamlet.

    c. In literature, two kinds of characters enhance the development of a story.

_____6. Which statement could serve as a main idea for the other two?

    a. The superb talent of individual players, such as Green Bay Packer Bret Favre or Tampa Bay Buccaneer Warren Sapp, creates excitement and fosters fan loyalty.

    b. Professional football's popularity is built on individual and team achievement.

    c. The Saints defeated the Colts in the 2010 Super Bowl, making this their first Super Bowl win and their very first Super Bowl appearance.

Directions: Read the paragraphs and answer the questions that follow.

[1]Many parents and teachers mishandle the use of praise by using evaluative praise rather than descriptive praise. [2]Evaluative praise makes a judgment about the child's behavior, which creates a need for approval and thus leads to dependence on the opinion of others. [3]For example, the evaluative praise statement "You are a marvelous student" focuses on the feelings and opinion of the one giving the praise. [4]In contrast, descriptive praise objectively describes the behavior and its positive effect. [5]This type of praise teaches the child to self evaluate. [6]For example, the descriptive praise statement "You have expert control of grammar rules, and you have a clear thesis that is well supported" allows the child to come to her own conclusions about her strengths as a writer. [7]Descriptive praise may require more effort, but it is much more effective than evaluative praise.

_____ 7. The topic of the paragraph is _____.

    a. judging a child's behavior

    b. evaluative and descriptive praise

    c. praising children and students

_____ 8. The main idea of the paragraph is stated in _____.

    a. sentence 1

    (b) sentence 2

    c. sentence 3

    d. sentence 4

[1]Conflicts emerge as a series of actions and reactions. [2]The "He did X and then she said Y and then he said Z and then . . ." formula is often used to explain a quarrel. [3]When incompatibilities arise people try to cope with them. [4]The way in which their actions mesh plays an important role in the direction the conflict takes. [5]Moves and countermoves depend on participants' ability and willingness to exert power. [6]Power can be defined as the capacity to act effectively. [7]Power sometimes takes the form of outward strength, status, money, or allies, but these are only the most obvious sources of power. [8]There are many other sources like time, attractiveness, and persuasive ability that operate in a much more subtle fashion.

—Folger, Peale, and Stutman, *Working Through Conflict*, 4th ed., p. 27.

_____ 9. The topic of the paragraph is _____.

    a. conflicts

    b. strength, status, money, and allies

    c. explanations of quarrels

    d. actions and reactions in conflict

_____ 10. The main idea of the paragraph is stated in _____.

    a. sentence 1

    b. sentence 2

    c. sentence 3

    d. sentence 4

Chapter 3: Stated Main Ideas
LAB 3.2 PRACTICE EXERCISE 2

Name_____ Section _____ Date _____ Score (number correct) _____ x 10 = _____

Objective: To determine topics and main ideas of paragraphs.

Directions: Read the paragraphs and answer the questions that follow.

Paragraph A

[1]Most human societies of the past were non-literate, which meant that they transmitted knowledge and history by word of mouth. [2]Written records are the most comprehensive source of information about the past, but they usually follow a strictly linear chronology. [3]They also served as educational tools. [4]Apart from anything else, written documents were useful cues for people to memorize standardized historical, ritual, or mythical information.

— Adapted from Fagan, *People of the Earth*, 9th ed., pp. 12–13.

____ 1. The topic of the paragraph is _____.
    a. human societies
    b. written records
    c. written documents about myths
    d. educational tools

____ 2. The main idea of the paragraph is stated in _____.
    a. sentence 1
    b. sentence 2
    c. sentence 3
    d. sentence 4

Paragraph B

[1]The Aztec oral histories, partially set down after the Spanish Conquest of the fifteenth century A.D., are an excellent example of history transmitted by word of mouth. [2]These oral histories were recited according to a well-defined narrative plot, which focused on great men as well as key events, like the dedication of the sun god Huitzilopochtli's temple in the Aztec capital in 1487. [3]The histories of favored groups were also predominant. [4]In these, as in other oral histories, there were formulas and themes which formed the central ingredients of a story that varied considerably from one speaker to the next even if the essential content was the same.

— Adapted from Fagan, *People of the Earth*, 9th ed., p. 13.

____ 3. The topic of the paragraph is _____.
    a. Hitzilopochtli's temple
    b. great men of Aztec oral histories
    c. oral histories
    d. Aztec oral histories

____ 4. The main idea of the paragraph is stated in _____.
    a. sentence 1
    b. sentence 2
    c. sentence 3
    d. sentence 4

Paragraph C

[1]If one individual has influenced research on child development more than any other, it is Swiss cognitive theorist Jean Piaget (1896–1980). [2]North American investigators had been aware of Piaget's work since 1930, mainly because his ideas were very much at odds with behaviorism, which dominated psychology during the middle of the twentieth century (Ziglar & Gilman, 1998). [3]Piaget did not believe that knowledge could be imposed on a reinforced child. [4]According to his cognitive-development theory, children actively construct knowledge as they manipulate and explore their world.

— Adapted from Berk, *Development Through the Lifespan*, 3rd ed., p. 19.

_____ 5. The topic of the paragraph is _____.
   a. psychology
   b. Jean Piaget and his cognitive-development theory
   c. twentieth-century behaviorism
   d. acquisition of knowledge

_____ 6. The main idea of the paragraph is stated in _____.
   a. sentence 1
   b. sentence 2
   c. sentence 3
   d. sentence 4

Paragraph D

[1]One library refused to circulate a novel—widely hailed by critics—because of the word *breast* (as in the sentence "Beneath this breast is a heart turned to stone"). [2]William Golding's novel *Lord of the Flies* raised more than a few eyebrows because it showed a group of English choirboys, cast away on a desert island, gradually losing their civilized veneer and becoming savages in their struggle to survive. [3]Richard Wright's *Native Son*, about an African American unjustly accused of a crime and unjustly treated in a white environment, won the Pulitzer Prize but was banned in many places. [4]Llian Smith's *Strange Fruit*, the first major novel to treat interracial love sympathetically, was unavailable in many bookstores and libraries after its publication. [5]Thus, books have been severely criticized, even banned, because of objectionable subject matter, characters, even individual words.

— Adapted from Janaro and Altshuler, *The Art of Being Human*, 7th ed., p. 540.

_____ 7. The topic of the paragraph is _____.
   a. *Lord of the Flies*
   b. interracial love
   c. Pulitzer Prize winners
   d. censoring of books

_____ 8. The main idea of the paragraph is stated in _____.
   a. sentence 1
   b. sentence 2
   c. sentence 3
   d. sentence 5

33

Paragraph E

[1]Because society is not a monolith, almost always an artist somewhere is being opposed, and the result can sometimes be artistically inhibiting, as in the case of Michael Cimino. [2]In 1978 Cimino directed *The Deer Hunter,* a film about a Vietnam War veteran's difficulties in readjusting to civilian life. [3]After it won the Academy Award as best picture, the director's stock went up immediately, and he had no trouble getting studio support as well as a big budget for his next venture, *Heaven's Gate.* [4]Although it won admirers elsewhere, in the United States it was destroyed by critics, who complained of its excessive length, its lack of plot and structure, and its self-indulgent style. [5]Cimino waited five years for another job, but by that time he was discouraged and afraid to make the bold directing choices for which *The Deer Hunter* was celebrated. [6]In attempting to please, he lost heart and altogether stopped expressing himself through cinema art.

— Adapted from Janaro and Altshuler, *The Art of Being Human,* 7th ed., p. 540.

_____ 9.   The topic of the paragraph is _____.
  a.   the success of Michael Cimino
  b.   the destructive results of artistic criticism
  c.   award-winning films
  d.   monoliths

_____ 10.   The main idea of the paragraph is stated in _____.
  a.   sentence 1
  b.   sentence 2
  c.   sentence 3
  d.   sentence 6

34

Chapter 3: Stated Main Ideas
LAB 3.3 REVIEW TEST 1

Name _____ Section _____ Date _____ Score (number correct) _____ x 10 = _____

Directions: Read the following passages and answer the questions that follow.

Passage A

[1]Watch preschoolers as they go about their daily activities, and you will see that they frequently talk out loud to themselves. [2]For example, as Sammy worked a puzzle, he said, "Where's the red piece? Now, a blue one. No, it doesn't fit. Try it here."

[3]Piaget (1923/1926) called these utterances *egocentric speech,* reflecting his belief that young children have difficulty taking the perspectives of others. [4]For this reason, he said, their talk is often "talk for self" in which they run off thoughts in whatever form they happen to occur, regardless of whether a listener can understand. [5]Piaget believed that cognitive maturity and certain social experiences— namely, disagreements with peers—eventually bring an end to egocentric speech. [6]Through arguments with agemates, children repeatedly see that others hold viewpoints different from their own. [7]As a result, egocentric speech declines.

[8]Vygotsky (1934/1987) voiced a powerful objection to Piaget's conclusions. [9]He reasoned that children speak to themselves for self-guidance. [10]Because language helps children think about their mental activities and behavior and select courses of action, Vygotsky viewed it as the foundation for all higher cognitive processes, including controlled attention, deliberative memorization and recall, categorization, planning, problem solving, and self-reflection. [11]As children get older and find tasks easier, their self-directed speech is internalized as silent, *inner speech*—the verbal dialogues we carry on with ourselves while thinking and acting in everyday situations.

[12]Over the past three decades, almost all studies have supported Vygotsky's perspective. [13]As a result, children's self-directed speech is now called *private speech* instead of egocentric speech. [14]Research shows that children use more of it when tasks are difficult and they are confused about how to proceed. [15]Also, as Vygotsky predicted, private speech goes underground with age, changing into whispers and silent lip movements (Duncan & Pratt, 1997; Patrick & Abravanel, 2000). [16]Finally, children who freely use speech during a challenging activity are more attentive and involved and do better than their less talkative agemates (Berk & Spuhl, 1995; Winser, Diaz, & Montero, 1997).

— Adapted from Berk, *Development Through the Lifespan*, 3rd ed., p. 223.

____ 1. The topic of the passage is _____.
   a. Piaget and egocentric speech
   b. Vygotsky's objections to Piaget's philosophies
   c. the inner speech of older children
   d. self-directed speech, or private speech, of children

____ 2. The central idea of the passage is expressed in the thesis statement, which is _____.
   a. sentence 3   b. sentence 8   c. sentence 11   d sentence 13

_____ 3. The topic of paragraph 1 is _____.
  a. preschoolers
  b. activities of preschoolers
  c. speech of preschoolers
  d. preschoolers at play

_____ 4. The main idea of paragraph 1 is expressed in which of the following sentences?
  a. Watch preschoolers as they go about their daily activities, and you will see that they frequently talk out loud to themselves
  b. Where's the red piece?
  c. Now, a blue one.
  d. No, it doesn't fit.

_____ 5. The topic of the paragraph 2 is _____.
  a. egocentric speech
  b. Piaget
  c. cognitive maturity
  d. argument of agemates

_____ 6. The main idea of paragraph 2 is expressed in which sentence?
  a. sentence 3
  b. sentence 4
  c. sentence 5
  d. sentence 6

_____ 7. The topic of paragraph 3 is _____.
  a. self-guidance
  b. Vygotsky's view
  c. inner speech
  d. higher cognitive processes

_____ 8. The main idea of paragraph 3 is expressed in _____.
  a. sentence 8
  b. sentence 9
  c. sentence 10
  d. sentence 11

_____ 9. The topic of paragraph 4 is _____.
  a. research
  b. early childhood
  c. egocentric speech
  d. private speech

___ 10. The main idea of paragraph 4 is expressed in _____.
  a. sentence 12
  b. sentence 13
  c. sentence 14
  d. sentence 16

Chapter 3: Stated Main Ideas
LAB 3.4 REVIEW TEST 2

Name _____ Section _____ Date _____ Score (number correct) _____ x 10 = _____

Directions: Consider the following sets of ideas. Two are specific statements that support the general main idea statement. Select the statement that could serve as a topic sentence for the other two.

_____ 1. Which sentence best serves as the main idea for the other two?
   a. Power walking burns calories and raises the heart rate without straining joints.
   b. Power walking has emotional and physical benefits.
   c. Power walking also helps to release stress and produce a sense of emotional wellbeing.

_____ 2. Which sentence best serves as the main idea for the other two?
   a. Cardiopulmonary resuscitation (CPR) is a low-cost lifesaving technique for heart attack victims.
   b. CPR involves rescue breathing (mouth-to-mouth resuscitation) alternating with pressure applied to the chest.
   c. It has been estimated that if one of every three Americans were trained in CPR, more than one hundred thousand lives a year could be saved.

_____ 3. Which sentence best serves as the main idea for the other two?
   a. ADHD is characterized by agitated behavior and an inability to focus on tasks.
   b. Ritalin is a medication prescribed for individuals who have an abnormally high level of activity or attention-deficit hyperactivity disorder (ADHD).
   c. Ritalin also is occasionally prescribed for treating narcolepsy, the sleeping disease.

_____ 4. Which sentence best serves as the main idea for the other two?
   a. Solar energy and water turbines are also becoming increasingly popular sources of electricity.
   b. Thousands of wind farms around the world are generating large amounts of electrical power.
   c. Rising energy prices are leading to the use of alternative sources of electricity.

Directions: Read each group of ideas and answer the questions that follow.

a. In 1993, Morrison was the first black woman to be awarded the Nobel Prize in literature.
b. American novelist Toni Morrison has won worldwide acclaim for her works that explore the black experience in a racist society.
c. Morrison's1988 novel *Beloved* earned her the Pulitzer Prize and established her as a major literary voice.

_____ 5. Statement (a) is _____.
   a. the main idea
   b. a supporting detail

_____ 6. Statement (b) is _____.
   a.   the main idea
   b.   a supporting detail

_____ 7. Statement (c) is _____.
   a.   the main idea
   b.   a supporting detail

a.   The television sitcom *Frasier* achieved record-breaking success.
b.   The sitcom made history by winning the Emmy for Outstanding Comedy Series five years in a row.
c.   In addition, Frasier, by its 11th season, set another industry record by winning a total of 31 Emmys.

_____ 8. Statement (a) is _____.
   a.   the main idea
   b.   a supporting detail

_____ 9. Statement (b) is _____.
   a.   the main idea
   b.   a supporting detail

___ 10. Statement (c) is _____.
   a.   the main idea
   b.   a supporting detail

Name_____ Section _____ Date _____ Score (number correct) _____ x 10 = _____

Directions: Read the following passages and answer the questions that follow.

Passage A

[1]Sex differences in motor skills are evident in early childhood. [2]Boys are slightly ahead of girls in skills that emphasize force and power. [3]By age five, they can jump slightly farther, run slightly faster, and throw a ball much farther (about five feet farther). [4]Girls have an edge in fine motor skills and in certain gross motor skills that require a combination of good balance and foot movement, such as hopping and skipping (Cratty, 1986; Thomas & French, 1985). [5]Boys' greater muscle mass and (in the case of throwing) slightly longer forearms may contribute to their skill advantages. [6]And girls' greater overall physical maturity may be partly responsible for their better balance and precision of movement.

[7]From an early age, boys and girls are usually channeled into different physical activities. [8]For example, fathers often play catch with their sons but seldom do so with their daughters. [9]Baseballs and footballs are purchased for boys, jump ropes and hula hoops for girls. [10]As children get older, sex differences in motor skills get larger, yet differences in physical capacity remain small until adolescence. [11]These trends suggest that social pressures for boys to be active and physically skilled and for girls to play quietly at fine motor activities may exaggerate small, genetically based sex differences (Croakley, 1990; Greeddorfer, Lewko, & Rosengren, 1996).

— Adapted from Berk, *Development through the Lifespan*, 3rd ed., p. 215

_____ 1. The central idea of the selection is _____.
   a. gross motor skills in boys
   b. fine motor skills in girls
   c. physical maturity in boys and girls
   d. sex differences in children's motor skills

_____ 2. The thesis statement of the selection is expressed in which sentence?
   a. Sex differences in motor skills are evident in early childhood.
   b. Girls have an edge in fine motor skills and in certain gross motor skills that require a combination of good balance and foot movement, such as hopping and skipping..
   c. Boys' greater muscle mass and (in the case of throwing) slightly longer forearms may contribute to their skill advantages.
   d. As children get older, sex differences in motor skills get larger, yet differences in physical capacity remain small until adolescence.

_____ 3. The main idea of paragraph 1 is expressed in _____.
   a. sentence 1
   b. sentence 2
   c. sentence 5
   d. sentence 6

_____ 4. The main idea of paragraph 2 is expressed in _____.
    a. sentence 8
    b. sentence 9
    c. sentence 10
    d. sentence 11

Passage B

[1]Contrary to what used to be taught, the humanities are not the record of the "best products of the best minds." [2]Those who advanced such a belief early in the 20th century may have done so in good faith, but they simply lacked information about _all the products of all the minds that ever existed._ [3]Sufficient information is still not available, but at least the problem has been brought out into the open. [4]Many of us keep trying to discover as much as we can about those who may have created works ignored or suppressed by powerful factions and those who were denied the opportunity to create anything.

[5]In Greek and Roman society women were either slaves or homemakers responsible for maintaining the "gracious" arts of civilized living. [6]These arts did not include fashioning statues out of heavy stone or carving the facades of public buildings. [7]In the Middle Ages the closest a woman could get to education was learning the duties and prayers of the sisterhood or, again, the gracious arts supervised by the lady of the castle. [8]These skills might include embroidery, tapestry weaving, and playing the lute, but never designing and installing a stained-glass window or painting a triptych on a church altar. [9]Consequently, these women never had an opportunity to learn or practice creative arts other than those needed for homemaking.

[10]During the 19th century, when a number of significant female novelists and poets _did_ emerge (although often with masculine pseudonyms), when education beyond home economics was no longer unheard of for a woman, training in musical composition, philosophy, and the visual arts was still considered a strictly masculine activity. [11]Although no one could have prevented a woman from privately composing music or from privately _thinking,_ there would have been no interested publishers.

[12]Virginia Woolf's title essay from _A Room of One's Own_ contrasted facilities offered to male and female students at Oxford University. [13]She was, for example, denied admission to a library reserved for men. [14]Nor were women allowed the privilege of living in a private room. [15]Many promising male talents attracted outside sponsors who paid their rent, an investment rarely made for a woman, even if she were equally talented. [16]Clearly, women were not given the same opportunities as men.

_____ 5. The topic of the passage is _____.
    a. Greek and Roman society
    b. female novelists of the 19th century
    c. a questionable view of the humanities as a record of the best works
    d. Virginia Woolf

_____ 6. The thesis statement of the selection is best expressed in which sentence?

    a. Contrary to what used to be taught, the humanities are not the record of the "best products of the best minds."

    b. Those who advanced such a belief early in the 20th century may have done so in good faith, but they simply lacked information about *all the products of all the minds that ever existed.*

    c. Many of us keep trying to discover as much as we can about those who may have created works ignored or suppressed by powerful factions and those who were denied the opportunity to create anything.

    d. Many promising male talents attracted outside sponsors who paid their rent, an investment rarely made for a woman, even if she were equally talented.

_____ 7. The topic of paragraph 2 is expressed in _____.

    a. sentence 5

    b. sentence 6

    c. sentence 8

    d. sentence 9

_____ 8. The topic of paragraph 3 is _____.

    a. the mergence of female novelists and poets in the 19th century

    b. the publishers' disinterest in women's artistic works in the 19th century

    c. higher education for women in the 19th century

    d. the domination by males of the visual arts in the 19th century

_____ 9. The topic of paragraph 4 is _____.

    a. the living facilities at Oxford University

    b. Virginia Woolf's university experiences

    c. the differing treatment of women at Oxford University

    d. the library privileges at Oxford University

_____ 10. The main idea of paragraph 4 is expressed in which sentence?

    a. sentence 12

    b. sentence 15

    c. sentence 15

    d. sentence 16

Chapter 3: Stated Main Ideas
LAB 3.6 MASTERY TEST 2

Name _____ Section _____ Date _____ Score (number correct) _____ x 10 = _____

Directions: Read the following passages and answer the questions that follow.

Passage A

[1]Societies can be classified by many features. [2]A popular classification of cultures is in terms of their masculinity and femininity (Hofstede, 1997, 1998). [3]In a highly "masculine" culture, men are viewed as assertive, oriented to material success, and strong; women, on the other hand, are viewed as modest, focused on the quality of life, and tender. [4]In a highly "feminine" culture, both men and women are encouraged to be modest, oriented to maintaining the quality of life, and tender. [5]The ten countries with the highest masculinity score (beginning with the highest) are Japan, Austria, Venezuela, Italy, Switzerland, Mexico, Ireland, Jamaica, Great Britain, and Germany. [6]The ten countries with the highest femininity score (beginning with the highest) are Sweden, Norway, Netherlands, Denmark, Costa Rica, Yugoslavia, Finland, Chile, Portugal, and Thailand. [7]Out of 53 countries ranked, the United States ranks 15th most masculine (Hofstede, 1997).

— Adapted from DeVito, *The Interpersonal Communication Book*, 10th ed. p. 45.

_____ 1. The topic of the paragraph is _____.
- a. popular cultures
- b. highly masculine cultures
- c. masculine and feminine societies
- d. highly feminine cultures

_____ 2. The main idea of the paragraph is _____.
- a. sentence 1
- b. sentence 2
- c. sentence 3
- d. sentence 4

Passage B

[1]Societies are not the only groups that sociologists classify. [2]Organizations can also be viewed in terms of masculinity or femininity. [3]Masculine organizations emphasize competitiveness and aggressiveness. [4]They focus on the bottom line and reward their workers on the basis of their contributions to the organization. [5]Feminine organizations are less competitive and less aggressive. [6]They're more likely to emphasize worker satisfaction and reward their workers on the basis of need; those who have large families, for example, may get better raises than the single people, even if the singles have contributed more to the organization.

—Adapted from DeVito, *The Interpersonal Communication Book*, 10th ed. p. 45.

_____ 3. The topic of the paragraph is _____.
- a. classifying societies
- b. competitiveness and aggressiveness
- c. worker satisfaction
- d. masculine and feminine organizations

42

_____ 4. The main idea of the paragraph is _____.
    a. sentence 1
    b. sentence 2
    c. sentence 4
    d. sentence 5

Passage C

The Family as Training Ground for Aggressive Behavior

1 "1 can't control him, he's impossible," complained Nadine, Robbie's mother, to Leslie one day. When Leslie asked if Robbie might be troubled by something going on at home, she discovered Robbie's parents fought constantly and resorted to harsh, inconsistent discipline. The same childrearing practices that undermine moral internalization—love withdrawal, power assertion, physical punishment, and inconsistency—are linked to aggression from early childhood through adolescence, in children of both sexes (Coie & Dodge, 1998; Stormshak et al., 2000).

2 Observations in families like Robbie's reveal that anger and punitiveness quickly create a conflict-ridden family atmosphere and an "out-of-control" child. The pattern begins with forceful discipline, which occurs more often with stressful life experiences, a parent's unstable personality, or a temperamentally difficult child. Once the parent threatens, criticizes, and punishes, the child whines, yells, and refuses until the parent "gives in." As these cycles become more frequent, they generate anxiety and irritability among other family members, who soon join in the hostile interactions (Patterson, 1997). Compared with siblings in typical families, preschool siblings who have critical, punitive parents are more verbally and physically aggressive to one another. Destructive sibling conflict, in turn, contributes to poor impulse control and antisocial behavior by the early school years (Garcia et al., 2000).

3 Because they are more active and impulsive and therefore harder to control, boys are more likely than girls to be targets of harsh, inconsistent discipline. Children who are products of these family processes soon view the world from a violent perspective, seeing hostile intent where it does not exist (Weiss et al., 1992). As a result, they make many unprovoked attacks. Soon they conclude that aggression "works" to control others. These cognitions contribute to the aggressive cycle (Egan, Monson, & Perry, 1998).

4 Highly aggressive children tend to be rejected by peers, to fail in school, and (by adolescence) to seek out deviant peer groups, which lead them toward violent delinquency and adult criminality.

5 Treatment for aggressive children must begin early, before their antisocial behavior becomes so well practiced that it is difficult to change. Breaking the cycle of hostilities between family members and replacing it with effective interaction styles are crucial. Leslie suggested that Robbie's parents see a family therapist, who observed their inept practices and coached them in alternatives. They learned not to give in to Robbie, to pair commands with reasons, and to replace verbal insults and spankings with more effective punishments, such as time out and withdrawal of privileges (Patterson, 1982). The therapist also encouraged Robbie's parents to be warmer and to give him attention and approval for prosocial acts.

6 At the same time, Leslie began teaching Robbie more successful ways of relating to peers. As opportunities arose, she encouraged Robbie to talk about a playmate's feelings and express his own. This helped Robbie take the perspective of others, empathize, and feel sympathetic concern (Denham, 1998). Robbie also participated in social problem-solving training. Over several months, he met with Leslie and a small group of classmates to act out common conflicts with puppets, discuss effective and ineffective ways of resolving them, and practice successful strategies. Children who receive such training show gains in social competency still present several months later (Shure, 1997). Finally, Robbie's parents got help with their marital problems. This, in addition to their improved ability to manage Robbie's behavior, greatly reduced tension and conflict in the household.

—Adapted from Berk, *Development Through the Lifespan*, 3rd ed., pp. 257–259.

_____ 5. The subject of this passage is _____.
   a. causes and treatment for aggressive behavior in children
   b. poor parenting
   c. effects of punishment
   d. antisocial behavior

_____ 6. A good title for paragraphs 1 through 4 would be _____.
   a. The Changing American Family
   b. The Family as Training Ground for Aggressive Behavior
   c. Cycles in the Typical American Family
   d. Antisocial Behavior

_____ 7. Which sentence states the thesis for paragraphs 1 through 4?
   a. "I can't control him, he's impossible," complained Nadine, Robbie's mother, to Leslie one day.
   b. When Leslie asked if Robbie might be troubled by something going on at home, she discovered Robbie's parents fought constantly and resorted to harsh, inconsistent discipline.
   c. The same childrearing practices that undermine moral internalization—love withdrawal, power assertion, physical punishment, and inconsistency—are linked to aggression from early childhood through adolescence, in children of both sexes.
   d. Robbie and his mother need some counseling

_____ 8. Which statement is the topic sentence for paragraph 2?
   a. Observations in families like Robbie's reveal that anger and punitiveness quickly create a conflict-ridden family atmosphere and an "out-of-control" child.
   b. Once the parent threatens, criticizes, and punishes, the child whines, yells, and refuses until the parent "gives in."
   c. The pattern begins with forceful discipline, which occurs more often with stressful life experiences, a parent's unstable personality, or a temperamentally difficult child.
   d. Destructive sibling conflict, in turn, contributes to poor impulse control and antisocial behavior by the early school years.

____ 9. A good title for paragraphs 5 through 7 would be _____.
     a. Helping Children and Parents Control Aggression
     b. Aggression in American Society
     c. Dealing with Aggressive Adults
     d. Children and a Cry for Help

____ 10. Which sentence is the thesis for paragraphs 5 through 7?
     a. Treatment for aggressive children must begin early, before their antisocial behavior becomes so well practiced that it is difficult to change.
     b. Breaking the cycle of hostilities between family members and replacing it with effective interaction styles are crucial.
     c. Leslie suggested that Robbie's parents see a family therapist, who observed their inept practices and coached them in alternatives.
     d. They learned not to give in to Robbie, to pair commands with reasons, and to replace verbal insults and spankings with more effective punishments, such as time out and withdrawal of privileges.

Chapter 4: Implied Main Ideas and Implied Central Ideas
LAB 4.1 PRACTICE EXERCISE 1

Name_____ Section _____ Date _____ Score (number correct) _____ x 10 = _____

Objective: To determine the implied main ideas and central idea.

A. Directions: Read each group of supporting details. Then, choose the best implied main idea.

Supporting details:
- Mindy refuses to eat in front of other people.
- Mindy often flushes her food down the toilet or throws it away when no one is looking.
- When Mindy does eat, she forces herself to throw up before the food can digest.
- Mindy, age 22, weighs 80 pounds and is 5 feet 4 inches in height. Mindy thinks she is fat.

_____1. Which sentence is the best statement of the implied main idea?
   a. Mindy is a healthy young woman.
   b. Mindy has a serious eating disorder.
   c. Mindy thinks she is fat.
   d. Mindy has low self-esteem.

- Commercial radio stations seek to make a profit, and programming is usually music, interview and call-in shows, and news.
- State-run radio stations are owned and operated by governments with direct control of content on a day-to-day basis.
- Public radio stations are noncommercial stations that receive money from the general public, private foundations, and governments.
- Shortwave radio beams international programming.
- Educational radio stations are owned and operated by universities, colleges, and even high schools; more than 800 U.S. educational institutions have broadcast licenses.
- Community radio stations are low-power stations that promote community participation in solving local problems.
- Special-interest radio stations are financed by noncommercial groups that have specific political or religious beliefs.
- Pirate radio stations are unlicensed stations.

—Adapted from Folkerts and Lacy, *The Media in Your Life*, 2001, p. 192.

_____ 2. Which sentence is the best statement of the implied main idea?
   a. The government supports many radio stations.
   b. The federal government licenses all radio stations.
   c. Radio stations can be divided into eight types on the basis of ownership and types of financing.
   d. Radio stations are an important part of modern society.

Directions: Read each paragraph. Then, choose the best implied main idea.

The most recent National Health and Nutrition survey indicated that only 8 percent of Americans consumed three or more servings of whole grains each day. Most experts believe that Americans should double their current consumption of dietary fiber—to 20 to 35 grams per day for most people and perhaps to 40 to 50 grams for others. (A large bowl of high fiber cereal with a banana provides close to 20 grams.)

—Adapted from Donatelle, *Health: the Basics*, 8th ed., p. 262.

_____ 3. Which sentence is the best statement of the implied main idea?
   a. Americans lack understanding of basic nutritional needs.
   b. Americans are consuming too many fats in their diet.
   c. Bananas are the best source of fiber.
   d. In spite of a growing amount of evidence supporting the benefits of high-fiber diets, most Americans are consuming too little fiber.

Yesenia, at one time, had a habit of thinking and saying negative thoughts about herself, such as, I am so stupid, I can't do this, and I am so fat (even though she was far from being overweight). During this time, she also felt a general and constant sense of anxiety, fear, and depression. Then one day several years ago, her friend Miguel chided her always being so negative about herself. "You know, Yesenia," he said, "You have a bad habit of bad-mouthing yourself. You would never talk about anyone as meanly as you talk about yourself. Give yourself a break by being nice to yourself. Be your own friend." Miguel's words made sense to Yesenia, and she began the process of changing her habit of negative self-talk. She created several positive statements about herself that she could use in place of the negative statements, such as "I have a good mind, I can figure this out," "I can do this," and "I have a curvy figure." Then, every time she began to say or think negative thoughts about herself, she substituted a positive statement. Gradually, her thoughts and speech changed, and her general sense of well-being improved.

_____ 4. Which sentence is the best statement of the implied main idea?
   a. Yesenia had low self-esteem.
   b. Miguel was a good friend to Yesenia.
   c. Yesenia had a bad habit that had to be changed.
   d. Yesenia changed the habitual self-talk that influenced her sense of well-being.

Jarrod sat in the back of the class with his notebook and textbooks open. He seemed bored during lectures, rarely took notes based on the teacher's instruction, and constantly flipped through his books, pausing frequently to read. When the instructor called on him to answer questions, he usually had to ask her to repeat the question. He then replied with the correct answer. He often challenged his teacher's feedback on his essays, forcing her to explain verbally her written remarks. His favorite classroom activities included using the computer to research, write, and revise his essays.

_____ 5. Which sentence is the best statement of the implied main idea?
   a. Jarrod did not like his instructor.
   b. Jarrod was an independent and active learner.
   c. Jarrod was a poor student.
   d. Jarrod paid attention to his instructor's feedback.

Marissa had worked for three weeks on her research project. She had used her home computer to locate a wide variety of government and educational sources for her topic. She had carefully followed her teacher's directions to create an outline, title page, and proper documentation. The night before the paper was due, Marissa was going over her project one last time to proofread for careless errors. Unexpectedly, a loud clap of thunder shook the walls, and lightning flashed just moments before her electricity cut off. Once power was restored, Marissa discovered that her computer had been severely damaged by the lightning strike, and her entire research project was wiped out. She had not made a backup copy on a disc or CD. Weeks of work were lost, and her grade was in jeopardy.

_____ 6. Which sentence is the best statement of the implied main idea?
    a. Lightning can cause major damage.
    b. Marissa is an excellent student who deserves an extension on the deadline for her research project.
    c. Marissa's story is an example of the need to always make backup copies of important work on a disc or CD.
    d. Computers can be frustrating.

Counters groan with creamy hunks of artisanal cheese. Medjool dates beckon amid rows of exotic fruit. Savory breads rest near fruit-drenched pastries, and prepared dishes like sesame-encrusted tuna rival what's sold in fine restaurants. Most of the store's goods carry labels proclaiming "organic," "100% natural," and "contains no additives." Staff people smile, happy to suggest wines that go with a particular cheese, or pause to debate the virtues of peanut butter maltballs. And it's all done against a backdrop of eye-pleasing earth-tone hues and soft lighting. This is grocery shopping?

—Adapted from Kotler and Armstrong, *Principles of Marketing*, 13th ed., p. 379.

_____ 7. Which sentence is the best statement of the implied main idea?
    a. This grocery store cultivates an "upscale" shopping experience that is different from that of most groceries stores.
    b. This is a discount grocery store.
    c. Grocery shopping is a frustrating experience for most people.
    d. Organic and natural foods are the best choice when shopping for groceries.

Sexual Harassment: An Abuse of Power

Although seldom a violent crime, sexual harassment is a criminal offense. Involving the abuse of power, it is found on the job, in the classroom, and in some cases, at home. It may be obvious, as in the case of a boss or professor imposing unwanted sexual attention or request for sexual favors. It may also be less direct, such as the creation of a hostile, intimidating, or offensive work or class environment by actions or speech of a sexual nature based on gender. On the college campus, sexual harassment might take the form of offers of a good grade in a course or special treatment in exchange for sexual favors, repeated staring in a suggestive way, or unwanted touching. Even sexual comments, jokes, or personal questions that are offensive or distracting to the person who feels harassed may be sexual harassment.

Most commonly, it is women who are harassed, usually by men in a position of power or authority over them. However, men may be harassed by women, and either men or women may be harassed by persons of the same sex. If harassers are left unchallenged, others may become victims because harassers are usually repeat offenders.

—Adapted from Pruitt and Stein, *HealthStyles*, 2nd ed., pp. 278–79

_____ 8. Which sentence best states the implied main idea of the first paragraph?
   a. Sexual harassment may be indirect, not always involving an explicit demand for sexual favors.
   b. College coeds are more susceptible to sexual harassment.
   c. Sexual harassment involves the abuse of power and can occur almost anywhere and in many ways.
   d. Sexual harassment is difficult to prove because it can involve so many types of behaviors.

_____ 9. Which sentence best states the implied main idea of the second paragraph?
   a. Sexual harassment is usually directed against women.
   b. Sexual harassment may be directed against men.
   c. Men or women may be sexually harassed by persons of the same sex.
   d. Sexual harassers are often repeat offenders and may victimize any person of any gender.

_____ 10. Which sentence best states the implied central idea of the passage?
   a. Sexual harassment is most often a violent crime directed against women.
   b. Sexual harassment, an abuse of power often by repeat offenders, is a criminal offense that can be directed against anyone.
   c. Sexual harassment is all about power.
   d. Sexual harassers should receive the counseling they need in order to prevent this abuse from recurring.

Chapter 4: Implied Main Ideas and Implied Central Ideas
LAB 4.2 PRACTICE EXERCISE 2

Name _____ Section _____ Date _____ Score (number correct) _____ x 10 = _____

Directions: Read the following paragraphs; then choose the best statement of the implied main idea for each paragraph.

Biotechnology is any alteration of organisms, cells, or biological molecules to achieve specific practical goals. For example, people have been using yeast cells to produce bread, beer, and wine for the past 10,000 years. Selectively breeding plants and animals that have desirable traits—crops that bear large fruits, docile cattle that grow rapidly and give lots of milk, cooperative dogs that protect and herd sheep— has an equally long history.

—Adapted from Audesirk, Audesirk, and Byers, *Life on Earth*, 5th ed., p. 188.

_____ 1. What is the best statement of the implied main idea?
   a. Biotechnology is a new area of science that is just now changing the world.
   b. Biotechnology is not a new science.
   c. The making of beer dates back to over 10,000 years.
   d. Scientists can now selectively breed plants and animals in order to produce the most desirable traits.

Expectant couples who are unhappy in their marriages and who have difficulty working out their differences continue to be distant, dissatisfied, and poor problem solvers after the baby is born (Cowan & Cowan, 2000; Curran et al., 2005). If their own parental relationships are mixed or negative, expectant mothers and fathers may have trouble building a healthy picture of themselves as parents. In a troubled marriage, pregnancy adds to rather than lessens family conflict (Perren et al., 2005).

_____ 2. What is the best statement of the implied main idea?
   a. Expectant parents must adjust their established roles to make room for children.
   b. Deciding to have a baby in hopes of improving a troubled relationship is a serious mistake.
   c. Babies are very demanding and can destroy a relationship.
   d. Couples with marital problems will be poor parents.

In the seventeenth century, French explorers had laid claim to the region between the Mississippi River and the Rocky Mountains, naming it Louisiana in honor of their king. The French wanted to block the British and the Spaniards from the area and also wanted to make sure that the port of New Orleans would remain in neutral hands. So, Napoleon sold Louisiana for $15 million to the United States in 1803, never having surveyed the area. The Louisiana Purchase doubled the land area of the new country.

—Adapted from Edgar, Hackett, Jewsbury, Molony, and Gordon, *Civilizations Past & Present, Vol. II, From 1300*, 12th ed., p. 652.

_____ 3. What is the best statement of the implied main idea?
   a. The French were some of the most resourceful explorers in the 1700s,
   b. The French proved their loyalty to their king in the naming of Louisiana.
   c. The United States doubled its size at a relatively small cost due to Napoleon's actions.
   d. The United States was considered a neutral country in the 1800s.

The most recent National Health and Nutrition survey indicated that only 8 percent of Americans consumed three or more servings of whole grains each day. Most experts believe that Americans should double their current consumption of dietary fiber—to 20 to 35 grams per day for most people and perhaps to 40 to 50 grams for others. (A large bowl of high fiber cereal with a banana provides close to 20 grams.)

—Adapted from Donatelle, *Health: the Basics*, 8th ed., p. 262.

_____ 4. What is the best statement of the implied main idea?
   a. Americans lack understanding of basic nutritional needs.
   b. Americans are consuming too many fats in their diet.
   c. Bananas are the best source of fiber.
   d. In spite of a growing amount of evidence supporting the benefits of a high-fiber diets, most Americans are consuming too little fiber.

Dealings with neighbors and relatives and involvement in church activities marked the outer limits of the social range of most Puritan women in the 1600s. Care of the children was a full-time job when broods of 12 or 14 were more common than those of one or two. Fewer children died in New England than in the Chesapeake or in Europe. Childbearing and motherhood, therefore, often lasted over two decades of a woman's life. Meanwhile, she also was the chief operating officer of the household. Cooking, baking, sewing, and supervising servants fell to her. In addition she had to master skills such as making cheese from milk, bacon from pork, and beer from malt. These jobs were physically demanding, yet large numbers of New England wives outlived one or more husbands.

—Adapted from Garraty and Carnes, *The American Nation, Volume I*, 10th ed., p. 52.

_____ 5. Which sentence is the best statement of the implied main idea?
   a. Puritan women in the 1600s were treated cruelly.
   b. Puritan women were strong and productive.
   c. American women today have a much easier life than Puritan women of the 1600s.
   d. Puritan women feared their husbands.

A growing number of people realize that divorce is a natural product of social change, and a majority are beginning to consider the divorced status "normal." Polls show that people believe divorce to be an acceptable solution to an unacceptable marriage. The women's movement has popularized the notion that it is all right for women to be independent and assertive and that men are not necessary to women's happiness. All these factors have made it easier for both partners, but for women especially, to seek a divorce instead of remaining in an unhappy marriage.

—Adapted from Perry and Perry, *Contemporary Society: An Introduction to Social Science*, 12th ed., p. 339.

_____ 6. Which sentence is the best statement of the implied main idea?
   a. Divorce is a natural part of change.
   b. It is better to be divorced than to remain in an unhappy marriage.
   c. Women are no longer dependent upon men.
   d. The prevalence of divorce has made it much more acceptable.

The Intergovernmental Panel on Climate Change (IPCC) report concludes that average surface temperatures on Earth increased by an estimated .74°C (1.33°F) in the century from 1906 to 2005, with most of this increase occurring in the last few decades. Eleven of the years from 1995 to 2006 were among the 12 warmest on record since global measurements began 150 years earlier. The numbers of extremely hot days and heat waves have increased, whereas the number of cold days has decreased.

—Withgott and Brennan, *Environment: The Science Behind the Stories*, 3rd. ed., p. 518.

_____ 7. Which sentence is the best statement of the implied main idea?
   a. The earth is gradually getting colder.
   b. The reason for the rise in earth's temperatures is a mystery.
   c. The rise in earth's temperatures will most likely continue.
   d. The IPCC is a nonscientific group who provides a watchdog service for the earth.

Directions. Read the following passage and answer the questions about the implied main idea.

Growth and Development of Public Speaking

Public speaking is a very old and a very new art. It's likely that public speaking principles were developed shortly after our species began to talk.

Aristotle's *Rhetoric*, written some 2,300 years ago in Greece, was one of the earliest well-thought-out studies of public speaking. It was in this work that the three kinds of proof were introduced: Logos are logical proofs, pathos are emotional appeals, and ethos are appeals based on the character of the speaker. This way of thinking about proofs is still used today. Romans added to the work of the Greeks. Quintillian taught in Rome during the first century and built an entire educational system based on the development of the effective and responsible public speaker or orator.

Throughout these 2,300 years, this Greco-Roman tradition has been deepened by experiments, surveys, field studies, and historical studies. Research has also added insights from other fields, mainly in the humanities and the social and behavioral sciences. And today, views from different cultures are blended into the study of public speaking.

—Adapted from DeVito, *Essentials of Human Communication*, 4th ed., p. 286.

_____ 8. Which sentence best states the implied main idea of the second paragraph?
   a. Aristotle developed a theory of proof 2,300 years ago that is still the basis of public speaking today.
   b. The Romans were interested in improving public speech as well.
   c. Public speakers need a thorough understanding of the history of speech.
   d. The Romans' education system focused on the development of effective public speaking skills.

_____ 9. Which sentence best states the implied main idea of the third paragraph?
   a. Public speaking has Greco-Roman roots.
   b. The humanities and social studies have contributed to the field of public speaking.
   c. Various cultures have had an influence on the art of public speaking.
   d. Public speaking has evolved over the years with input from many different areas.

_____ 10. What is the implied central idea of the passage?
   a. Public speaking is a difficult subject to learn.
   b. Public speaking has been studied since ancient times and has evolved over the years into a form of art.
   c. The Greco-Romans developed public speaking into an art form.
   d. Public speakers are required to do much study and research to be effective.

Name_____ Section _____ Date _____ Score (number correct) _____ x 10 = _____

A. Directions: Choose the best implied main idea of each paragraph.

In middle childhood, highly active children, especially boys, have just as much safety knowledge as their peers, but they are far less likely to implement it. Parents of these children tend to be particularly lax in intervening in the dangerous behaviors of such children. Furthermore, compared with girls, boys judge risky play activities as less likely to result in injury, and they pay less attention to injury risk cues, such as a peer who looks hesitant or fearful. The greatest challenge for injury-control programs is reaching these children, altering high-risk factors in their families, and reducing the dangers to which they are exposed.

—Adapted from Berk, *Infants and Children*, 6th ed., p. 424.

_____ 1.   What is the best statement of the implied main idea?
- a.   Highly active, impulsive children, many of whom are boys, are particularly susceptible to injury in middle childhood.
- b.   Parents of middle-aged school children typically do not pay attention to the safety of their children.
- c.   Boys tend to be more impulsive than girls.
- d.   Injury-control programs are necessary in order to keep children safe from harm.

Beginning in 1945, The Old Man of the Mountain, also known as The Great Stone Face, appeared at the center of the official state emblem. It was a natural rock formation sculpted from Conway Red Granite that, when viewed from the proper location, gave the appearance of an old man. Until it collapsed in 2003, each year hundreds of thousands of people traveled to view the Old Man, which protruded from high on Cannon Mountain, 360 meters (1,200 feet) above Profile Lake in northern New Hampshire's Franconia Notch State Park.

—Adapted from Tarbuck, Lutgens, and Tasa, *Earth Science*, 12th ed., p. 88.

_____ 2.   What is the best statement of the implied main idea?
- a.   The Old Man of the Mountain was a natural rock foundation that collapsed in 2003.
- b.   The Old Man of the Mountain could be visited by traveling to Cannon Mountain, New Hampshire.
- c.   Until its collapse, The Old Man of the Mountain was one of New Hampshire's best-known state symbols.
- d.   New Hampshire's parks contain many wonderful sights for tourists.

In the past few decades, we have seen Chinese students clamoring for democracy, Eastern Europeans unhappy with their new governments, Russians lamenting the plight of their economy, Palestinians throwing rocks from the rooftops or blowing themselves up in suicide bombings. In the United States, too, on more than one occasion, we have seen the streets of our major cities erupt in violence that took many lives and destroyed whole neighborhoods. Sometimes, when a sports team wins an important victory, opposing groups of fans clash, and fights break out that may end in some persons' deaths. Traditional holidays, such as Halloween, have become occasions for mob violence in some locations.

—Adapted from Perry and Perry, *Contemporary Society: An Introduction to Social Science*, 12th ed., p. 274.

_____ 3. What is the best statement of the implied main idea?
   a. The sports arena has become too violent, encouraging fans and players alike to clash against their rivals.
   b. Suicide bombings first originated in Palestine and are becoming a common way of protest against one's enemies.
   c. The past decades have been filled with scenes of violence all around the world.
   d. Observance of Halloween as a national holiday should be discontinued because it encourages acts of violence.

Much of the vitamin E that we consume comes from vegetable oils and the products made from them. Safflower oil, sunflower oil, canola oil, and soybean oil are good sources of vitamin E. Mayonnaise and salad dressings made from these oils also contain vitamin E. Nuts, seeds, and some vegetables also contribute vitamin E to our diet. Although no single fruit or vegetable contains very high amounts of vitamin E, eating five to nine servings of fruits and vegetables along with other vitamin E-containing foods each day will help ensure adequate intake of this nutrient.

—Adapted from Thompson and Manore, *Nutrition: An Applied Approach*, 2nd ed., p. 310.

_____ 4. What is the best statement of the implied main idea?
   a. Vitamin E is important to our good health.
   b. Most people get enough of vitamin E because it is found in so many foods.
   c. Cooking oils are good sources for the important vitamin E.
   d. Everyone should eat plenty of fruits and vegetables a day to maintain a healthy diet.

Predator and prey populations exert intense natural selection on one another. As prey become more difficult to catch, predators must become more adept at hunting them, and as predators become more adept, prey must get better eluding them. Coevolution has thus endowed both the cheetah and its antelope prey with speed and camouflage. It has produced the keen eyesight of the hawk and the poisons and bright warning colors of the poison arrow frog and the coral snake.

—Adapted from Audesirk, Audesirk, and Byers, *Life on Earth*, 5th ed., p. 560.

_____ 5. What is the best statement of the implied main idea?
   a. Hunting food is becoming more and more difficult for wild animals as our civilization expands.
   b. Nature endows some creatures with bight warning colors to avoid being eaten.
   c. Coevolution has modified both predator and prey for survival.
   d. Coevolution has endowed the cheetah with great speed but provided the antelope with camouflage.

B. Directions: Read the following selection from *Mark Twain's Autobiography* and answer the questions that follow.

From "Memories of a Missouri Farm"
by Mark Twain

My parents removed to Missouri in the early thirties; I do not remember just when, for I was not born then and cared nothing for such things. It was a long journey in those days, and must have been a rough and tiresome one. The home was made in the wee village of Florida, in Monroe County, and I was born there in 1835. The village contained a hundred people and I increased the population by 1 percent. It is more than many of the best men in history could have done for a town. It may not be modest in me to refer to this, but it is true. There is no record of a person doing as much—not even Shakespeare. But I did it for Florida, and it shows that I could have done it for any place—even London, I suppose.

Recently some one in Missouri has sent me a picture of the house I was born in. Heretofore I have always stated that it was a palace, but I shall be more guarded now.

I used to remember my brother Henry walking into a fire outdoors when he was a week old. It was remarkable in me to remember a thing like that, and it was still more remarkable that I should cling to the delusion, for thirty years, that I *did* remember it—for of course it never happened; he would not have been able to walk at that age. If I had stopped to reflect, I should not have burdened my memory with that impossible rubbish so long. It is believed by many people that an impression deposited in a child's memory within the first two years of its life cannot remain there five years, but that is an error. The incident of Benvenuto Cellini and the salamander must be accepted as authentic and trustworthy; and then that remarkable and indisputable instance in the experience of Helen Keller—However, I will speak of that at another time. For many years I believed that I remembered helping my grandfather drink his whisky toddy when I was six weeks old, but I do not tell about that any more, now; I am grown old and my memory is not as active as it used to be. When I was younger I could remember anything, whether it had happened or not; but my faculties are decaying now, and soon I shall be so I cannot remember any but the things that never happened. It is sad to go to pieces like this, but we all have to do it.

—From *Mark Twain's Autobiography*. Copyright © 1924 by Clara Gabrilowitsch.

_____ 7. What is the best statement of the implied main idea of paragraph 1?
   a. Mark Twain wished he had been born in London.
   b. Mark Twain is poking fun at himself and his small hometown by taking pride in something that was not of his own making – his birth.
   c. Mark Twain was born in the 1930s.
   d. Mark Twain's parents were not very wealthy.

_____ 8. What is the best statement of the implied main idea of paragraph 2?
   a. Mark Twain could not remember the house where he was born.
   b. Mark Twain realized that his house was not as grand as he thought it was as a child.
   c. Mark Twain thought his house was grand because he had such an idyllic childhood.
   d. Mark Twain will have to stop telling stories about his childhood.

_____ 9. What is the best statement of the implied main idea of paragraph 3?
a. Mark Twain had a remarkable memory when he was young.
b. Mark Twain was a friend to Helen Keller.
c. Mark Twain's brother was in a tragic accident.
d. Mark Twain rues the fact that his memory never was very reliable, and now in his old age, it is even worse.

_____ 10. Which sentence best states the implied central idea?
a. Mark Twain enjoys making fun of himself.
b. Mark Twain often tells lies about himself.
c. Mark Twain knew many famous people.
d. Mark Twain's childhood was not very glamorous.

Chapter 4: Implied Main Ideas and Implied Central Ideas
LAB 4.4 REVIEW TEST 2

Name_____Section _____ Date _____ Score (number correct) _____ x 10 = _____

A. Directions: Read each group of supporting details. Then, choose the best implied main idea.

- In October, the festivities of Halloween require making or buying costumes and candy, as well as carving pumpkins and staging festivals or haunted houses.
- In November, hours of work go into buying, preparing, and serving Thanksgiving dinners for family and for those less fortunate.
- In December, people spend money and time shopping for and wrapping gifts, baking, decorating, hosting and attending parties in celebration of religious holidays such as Christmas and Hanukkah.
- In January, many people host or attend parties to celebrate the New Year.

_____ 1. Which sentence best expresses the implied main idea?
   a. Hours of work go into fall holidays.
   b. The fall and winter holidays are very busy times.
   c. The most important holidays occur during the winter.
   d. By January, most winter holidays have ended.

- The FTC turns up hundreds of Web sites touting unproven cures for cancer.
- One site pushes more than 100 alternative cancer treatments that it claims are safe, effective, and nontoxic.
- Types of cures for cancer include herbal teas and fish extracts—even electronic zappers.
- One site involved placing cancer patients in a series of comas over a seven-week period at a cost of nearly $40,000.

   —Adapted from Goldsmith, *Consumer Economics: Issues and Behaviors*, 2nd ed., p. 260.

_____ 2. Which sentence best expresses the implied main idea?
   a. The government should allow more alternative methods for curing cancer.
   b. Herbal teas and fish extracts are proven cures for many serious diseases.
   c. There are many fraudulent cures or remedies for cancer that take advantage of people who are susceptible as a result of having this disease.
   d. Cures for cancer are very expensive.

Take your new pet to a veterinarian as soon as possible and schedule regular check-ups for vaccinations and worm treatments. To ensure health, feed your pet a well-balanced diet and do not let the pet drink water from a toilet or eat raw food. Keep your pet's living area and bedding clean. Dispose of your pet's feces carefully by burying it or wrapping it in plastic before discarding in the trash; use plastic gloves and wash your hands immediately. Obey leash laws and monitor your pet's whereabouts to avoid risk of disease from exposure to wild animals.

____ 3. Which sentence is the best statement of the implied main idea?
   a. Most people can't handle the responsibility that comes with a pet.
   b. Pets need veterinarian care to routinely monitor their health.
   c. Cleaning up after pets requires sanitary practices for the good of the environment.
   d. Pets require much care to keep them healthy and safe.

If a chemical pollutant, collectively referred to as persistent organic pollutants (POPs), gets into the soil, a plant can absorb the chemical into its structure and can pass it on as part of the food chain. Animals can then absorb the pollutant into their tissues or can consume it when feeding on plants growing in the polluted soil. Fat-soluble pollutants are especially problematic, as they tend to accumulate in the animal's body tissues and are then absorbed by humans when the animal is used as a food source.

—Adapted from Thompson and Manore, *Nutrition for Life*, 2nd ed., p. 405.

____ 4. Which sentence is the best statement of the implied main idea?
   a. Persistent organic pollutants are harmful chemicals.
   b. Animals can absorb harmful chemicals into their tissues.
   c. Persistent organic pollutants can enter the food chain through the soil.
   d. Harmful chemicals that can endanger our food supply are a global concern.

The number of Internet users world-wide now stands at more than 1.2 billion and will reach an estimated 3.4 billion by 2015. Today's typical Internet users spend 47 percent of their time online looking at online content—watching video, reading the news, or getting the lowdown on friends and celebrities on MySpace or Facebook. They spend another 33 percent of their online time communicating with each other, 15 percent shopping, and 5 percent Googling or using other search engines.

—Adapted from Kotler and Armstrong, *Principles of Marketing*, 13th ed., p. 25.

____ 5. Which sentence is the best statement of the implied main idea?
   a. Computers and the Internet have become an indispensable part of our lives.
   b. People spend more time on Facebook than they spend on research.
   c. The average Internet users spend most of their time looking at online content.
   d. Internet use will continue to grow until 2015.

"Is it boy, or is it a girl?" Parents of babies send out different kinds of birth announcements based upon the answer to this question. Girl and boy babies are dressed in different clothes and wrapped in different-colored blankets. Parents even play with boy and girl babies differently: From birth, fathers tend to interact more with sons, while mothers interact more with daughters. Fathers typically engage in more physical, rough-and-tumble activities and mothers in traditional games such as peek-a-boo.

—Adapted from Feldman, *Child Development*, 5th ed., p. 175.

____ 6. Which sentence is the best statement of the implied main idea?
   a. From the moment of birth, girls and boys are treated differently.
   b. Fathers are typically more comfortable interacting with boy babies.
   c. Parents teach their children gender-specific behaviors from birth.
   d. Male infants tend to be more physically active than girl babies.

During sleep, chemicals that were used up during the day's activities are replenished and cellular damage is repaired. There is evidence that most bodily growth and repair occur during the deepest stages of sleep, when enzymes responsible for those functions are secreted in higher amounts. This may account for the fact that children in periods of rapid growth need to sleep more and also helps to explain why children who are experiencing disrupted sleep (as in the case in situations of domestic violence) suffer delays in growth.

—Adapted from Ciccarelli and White, *Psychology*, 2nd ed., p. 140.

_____ 7. Which sentence is the best statement of the implied main idea?
    a. Some people need more sleep than others.
    b. Children living in violent homes have disturbed sleep patterns.
    c. Sleep deprivation is a serious problem that many have without realizing it.
    d. Sleep is necessary to the physical health of the body.

Directions: Read this selection from a college history book and answer the questions that follow.

As the Reagan administration eased corporate access to the nation's natural resources in the 1980s, most Americans' real wages declined. The professional classes, however, fared well, and the wealthiest citizens gained enormously. For example, the salary of an average corporate chief executive officer was 40 times greater than that of a typical factory worker in 1980; by 1989, it was 93 times greater. The top 1 percent of American families now possessed more assets than the bottom 90 percent—a ratio typical of Third World nations.

A series of corporate mergers and consolidations as well as financial speculation and manipulation on Wall Street greatly contributed to this trend. This explosion of wealth at the top fueled an emerging culture of extravagance, reminiscent of similar trends in the late nineteenth century and in the 1920s. Newly identified "yuppies" (young urban professionals) embodied the drive for material acquisition.

As the **affluence gap** widened, the broad middle class watched its job security slip. Early in the decade, the recession had prompted factory shutdowns and mass layoffs. More than a million industrial jobs disappeared in 1982 alone. Manufacturers' decisions to keep moving plants abroad for cheaper labor only worsened the situation. The poorest Americans saw their already meager incomes decline by another 10 percent. In 1986 a full-time worker at minimum wage earned $6,700 per year—almost $4,000 short of the poverty level for a family of four. Homelessness worsened in cities as the government cut funding for welfare and institutional care for the mentally ill while housings costs rose. More than 1 million people lived on the streets, one-fifth of them still employed. One out of eight children went hungry and 20 percent lived in poverty. Meanwhile Congress and the White House provided large federal subsidies to "needy" businesses such as the Chrysler Corporation and the savings and loan industry.

—Adapted from Jones et al., Created Equal: *A History of the United States*, Combined Volume, brief 3rd ed., p. 643.

_____ 8. Which sentence best states the implied main idea of the first paragraph?
    a. Corporations received many benefits during Reagan's administration.
    b. The United States grew very similar to Third World nations during the 1980s.
    c. The wages of the wealthiest citizens and professional workers increased considerably in the 1980s compared to the wages of most Americans.
    d. Corporate chiefs and professional workers enjoyed large salary increases in the 1980s.

_____ 9. According to the information in the third paragraph, the phrase *affluence gap* most likely means
_____.
   a. a break in trust and confidence
   b. the unequal control of power
   c. the disproportionate ratio of wealth and material comfort between groups
   d. the disappearance of hope and belief in the government's ability to be fair to its citizens

_____ 10. Which sentence best states the implied central idea of the passage?
   a. During the 1980s, the difference in wages and living conditions between the very rich and the very poor increased immensely.
   b. The Reagan years were times of prosperity for the United States.
   c. The rise of corporations led to the downfall of the average American citizen during the 1980s.
   d. The 1980s were extremely difficult times for most Americans.

Chapter 4: Implied Main Ideas and Implied Central Ideas
LAB 4.5 MASTERY TEST 1

Name _____ Section _____ Date _____ Score (number correct) _____ x 10 = _____

A. Directions: Read each of the following paragraphs and choose the implied main idea.

Disease has always afflicted humans but its impact has varied throughout history. Archaeology indicates that early hunter-gatherers experienced relatively disease-free lives. The small size of hunter-gatherer communities, their isolation from one another, their nomadic lifestyle, and their omnivorous, varied diet all contributed to limiting the contraction and spread of disease. In a worst-case scenario, even if a single community were to be afflicted by an epidemic, the disease, however many individual lives it might claim, would likely run its course before it could be passed onto other communities.

—Adapted from Edgar, Hackett, Jewsbury, Molony, and Gordon, *Civilizations Past & Present, Vol. II, From 1300*, 12th ed., p. 418.

_____ 1. What is the best statement of the implied main idea?
    a. Our early ancestors were hunter-gatherers who primarily existed on meat.
    b. It is likely that disease played a less significant role in the lives of our distant ancestors than it does now.
    c. Disease claimed many lives of individual communities in our past.
    d. Advances in science have helped to control the spread of disease today, unlike our ancestors who had no such advantage.

Younger children often have difficulty with skills that require rapid responding, such as dribbling and batting. During middle childhood, the capacity to react only to relevant information increases and steady gains in reaction time occur, with 11-year olds responding twice as quickly as 5-year-olds. Because 6- and 7-year-olds are seldom successful at batting a thrown ball, T-ball is more appropriate for them than baseball. Similarly, handball, four-square, and kickball should precede instruction in tennis, basketball, and football.

—Adapted from Berk, *Infants and Children*, 6th ed., p. 428.

_____ 2. What is the best statement of the implied main idea?
    a. Differences in speed and reaction of children can have practical implications for physical education.
    b. Organized sports are too difficult for young children.
    c. Children should learn tennis, basketball, and football until they reach their middle years.
    d. Healthy infants don't experience problems playing appropriate sports for their age.

Underage drinking often results in crashes, violence, property crime, suicide, burns, drowning, fetal alcohol syndrome, high-risk sex, poisoning, psychoses, and treatments for alcohol dependence. The largest costs were related to violence ($34.7 billion) and drunken-driving accidents ($13.5 billion), following by high-risk sex (nearly $5 billion), property crime ($3 billion), and addiction treatment programs (nearly $2 billion). By dividing the cost of underage drinking by the estimated number of underage drinkers, one study estimated that every underage drinker costs society an average of $4,680 a year.

—Adapted from Donatelle, *Health: the Basics*, 8th ed., p. 230.

_____ 3. What is the best statement of the implied main idea?
   a. Underage drinking poses an enormous cost to society.
   b. Underage drinking most often results in violence.
   c. Laws need to be enforced to curtail underage drinking.
   d. More addiction-treatment programs are needed to treat underage drinkers.

C. Directions. Read the following passage and answer the questions that follow.

The Impact of Poverty

When families slip into poverty, development is seriously threatened. Consider the case of Zinnia Mae, who grew up in Trackton, a close-knit black community located in a small southeastern American city. As unemployment struck Trackton in the 1980s and citizens moved away, 16-year-old Zinnia Mae caught a ride to Atlanta. Two years later, Zinnia Mae was the mother of three children—a daughter and twin boys. She had moved into high-rise public housing.

Each of Zinnia Mae's days was much the same. She watched TV and talked with girlfriends on the phone. The children had only one set meal (breakfast) and otherwise ate whenever they were hungry or bored. Their play space was limited to the living-room sofa and a mattress on the floor. Toys consisted of scraps of a blanket, spoons and food cartons, a small rubber ball, a few plastic cars, and a roller skate abandoned in the building. Zinnia Mae's most frequent words were "I'm so tired." She worried about where to find baby-sitters so she could go to the laundry or grocery, and about what she would do if she located the twins' father, who had stopped sending money.

Over the past 30 years, economic changes in the United States and Canada have caused the poverty rate to climb substantially; in recent years, it has dropped and then risen again. Today, nearly 12 percent of the population in the United States and Canada are affected. Those hit hardest are parents under age 25 with young children and elderly people who live alone. Poverty is also magnified among ethnic minorities and women. For example, 17 percent of American and Canadian children are poor, a rate that climbs to 32 percent for Native American children, 34 percent for African American and Hispanic children, and 60 percent for Canadian Aboriginal children. (Aboriginal peoples in Canada include First Nations, Inuit, and Metis.) For single mothers with preschool children and elderly women on their own, the poverty rate in both countries is nearly 50 percent. (Canadian National Council of Welfare, 2002; U.S. Bureau of the Census, 2002c).

Joblessness, a high divorce rate, a lower remarriage rate among women than men, widowhood, and (as we will see later) inadequate government programs to meet family needs are responsible for those disheartening statistics. The child poverty rate is higher than that of any other age group. And of all Western nations, the United States has a higher percentage of extremely poor children. These circumstances are particularly worrisome because the earlier poverty begins, the deeper it is, and the longer it lasts, the more devastating its effects on physical and mental health and school achievement (Children's Defense Fund, 2003; Ziglar & Hall, 2000).

The constant stresses that accompany poverty gradually weaken the family system. Poor families have many daily hassles—bills to pay, the car breaking down, loss of welfare and unemployment payments, something stolen from the house, to name just a few. When daily crises arise, family members become depressed, irritable, and distracted, and hostile interactions increase (McLoyd, 1998). These outcomes are especially severe in families that must live in poor housing and dangerous neighborhoods—conditions that make everyday existence even more difficult, while reducing social supports that help people cope with economic hardship (Brooks-Gunn & Duncan, 1997).

—Berk, *Development Through the Lifespan*, 3rd ed., p. 64.

_____ 4. The topic of the passage is
   a. Zinna Mae
   b. the impact of poverty
   c. a typical day for Zinna Mae and her children
   d. joblessness and poverty

_____ 5. What is the stated main idea of paragraph 2?
   a. Each of Zinnia Mae's days was much the same.
   b. She watched TV and talked with girlfriends on the phone.
   c. The children had only one set meal (breakfast) and otherwise ate whenever they were hungry or bored.
   d. She worried about where to find baby-sitters so she could to the laundry or grocery, and about what she would do if she located the twins' father, who had stopped sending money.

_____ 6. What is the implied main idea of paragraph 4?
   a. The poverty rate in the United States and Canada is the result of several factors.
   b. Joblessness is one factor that causes poverty in the United States and Canada.
   c. Women are more often reported in the poverty statistics than men.
   d. The child poverty rate is higher in the United States than in Canada.

_____ 7. What is the implied main idea of paragraph 6?
   a. Poverty was an uncommon phenomenon 25 years ago.
   b. Homelessness was an uncommon phenomenon 25 years ago.
   c. Besides poverty, homelessness is another factor that has reduced the life chances of many children and adults.
   d. Mental illness is a major cause of homelessness.

_____ 8. What is the topic of paragraph 7?
   a. Homelessness
   b. Homeless families
   c. Homeless children
   d. Poverty-stricken school-age children

_____ 9. What is the implied main idea of paragraph 7?
   a. Most homeless families are single-parent families with a mother and children under the age of five.
   b. Homeless children suffer from health problems, developmental delays, and serious emotional stress.
   c. At least one-fourth of homeless school-age children do not attend school.
   d. Homeless children achieve less than other poor children.

_____ 10. What is the central idea of the selection?
   a. Poverty is a global problem all countries need to address.
   b. Education can help alleviate the problems of poverty.
   c. The poverty rate for children is higher than the poverty rate for any other age group in America.
   d. The United States and Canada have programs to eliminate poverty.

64

Name_____ Section _____ Date _____ Score (number correct) _____ x 10 = _____

A. Directions: Read each of the following paragraphs and choose the implied main idea.

Mothers who are experiencing high levels of stress are more likely to be punitive and negative toward their children, with resulting increases in the children's defiant and noncompliant behavior. Maternal negativity, in turn, is implicated in the persistence of noncompliant behavior into elementary school. This link is clear, for example, in Susan Campbell's longitudinal study of a group of noncompliant children. Campbell finds that among a group of three-year-olds who were labeled "hard to manage," those who had improved by age six had mothers who had been less negative.

—Adapted from Bee and Boyd, *The Developing Child*, 11th ed., p. 464.

_____ 1. Which sentence is the best statement of the implied main idea?
    a. Susan Campbell has completed a study of noncompliant children.
    b. Mothers who are negative are more inclined to use physical punishment.
    c. The mother's ability to support the child's development in the preschool years is affected by the amount of stress she is experiencing.
    d. When children reach three years of age, they typically become difficult to handle.

Current new treatments for HIV combine selected drugs, especially protease inhibitors and reverse transcriptase inhibitors. Protease inhibitors act to prevent the production of the virus in chronically infected cells that HIV has already invaded. Other drugs inhibit the HIV enzyme reverse transcriptase before the virus has invaded the cell, thereby preventing the virus from infecting new cells.

—Adapted from Donatelle, *Health: the Basics*, 8th ed., p. 409

_____ 2. Which sentence is the best statement of the implied main idea?
    a. New drugs are slowing the progression of HIV.
    b. HIV works by invading the cells of the body.
    c. HIV is a deadly disease from which almost no one recovers.
    d. Scientists still do not have a cure for HIV.

B. Directions: Read this selection from a college communications book and answer the questions that follow.

Your Basic Emotions

To capture the similarities among emotions, many researchers have tried to identify basic or primary emotions. Robert Plutchik (1980; Havlena, Holbrook, & Lehmann, 1989) developed a most helpful model. In this model there are eight basic emotions.

Figure 7.1

A Model of the Emotions

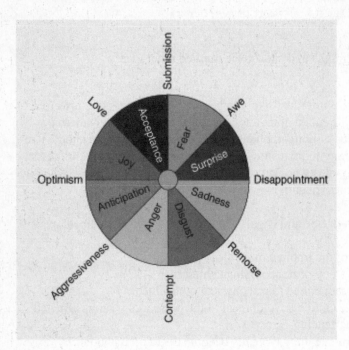

Source: From *Emotion: A Psychoevolutionary Synthesis* by Robert Plutchik. Copyright 1980 by Robert Plutchik. Reprinted by permission of HarperCollins Publishers, Inc.

The eight pieces of the pie represent the eight basic emotions: joy, acceptance, fear, surprise, sadness, disgust, anger, and anticipation. Emotions that are close to each other on this wheel are also close to each other in meaning. For example, joy and anticipation are more closely related than are joy and sadness or acceptance and disgust. Emotions that are opposite each other on the wheel are also opposite each other in their meaning. For example, joy is the opposite of sadness, anger is the opposite of fear.

In this model there are also blends. These are emotions that are combinations of the primary emotions. These are noted outside the emotion wheel. For example, according to this model, love is a blend of joy and acceptance. Remorse is a blend of disgust and sadness.

Emotional Arousal

If you were to describe the events leading up to emotional arousal, you would probably describe three stages: (1) an event occurs; (2) you experience an emotion: you feel surprise, joy, anger; (3) you respond physiologically: your heart beats faster, face flushes, and so on.

Psychologist William James and physiologist Carl Lange offered a different explanation. Their theory places the physiological arousal before the experience of the emotion. The James-Lange sequence is: (1) an event occurs; (2) you respond physiologically; and (3) you experience an emotion, for example, you feel joy or sadness.

Figure 7.2
Three Views of Emotion

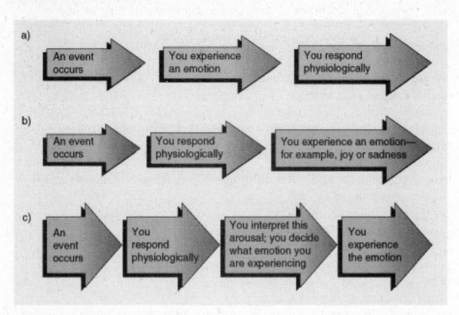

A third explanation is called the cognitive labeling theory (Schachter, 1964). According to this explanation, you interpret the physiological arousal and, on the basis of this, experience the emotions of joy, sadness, or whatever. The sequence of events goes like this: (1) an event occurs; (2) you respond physiologically; (3) you interpret this arousal—that is, you decide what emotion you're experiencing; and (4) you experience the emotion. Your interpretation of this arousal will depend on the situation you're in. For example, if you experience an increased pulse rate after someone you've been admiring smiles at you, you might interpret this as joy. You might, however, interpret that same increased heart beat as fear when three suspicious-looking strangers approach you on a dark street. It's only after you make this interpretation that you experience the emotion, for example, the joy or the fear.

—Adapted from DeVito, *Messages: Building Interpersonal Communication Skills*,
4th ed. pp. 174–175

_____ 3. The topic of the passage is _____.
  a. the similarities among emotions
  b. the eight basic emotions
  c. the three views of emotional arousal
  d. basic emotions and emotional arousal

_____ 4. Based on the figure labeled 7.1, the emotion of love is a combination of _____.
  a. awe and submission
  b. optimism and submission
  c. anticipation and joy
  d. joy and acceptance

67

_____ 5. The implied main idea of the first section of the passage entitled "Your Basic Emotions" is stated in which sentence?
   a. The Plutchik model of emotions illustrates the eight basic emotions and their emotional blends.
   b. The eight basic emotions include joy, acceptance, fear, sadness, disgust, anger, and anticipation.
   c. Blended emotions are combinations of the primary emotions.
   d. Remorse is a blend of disgust and sadness.

_____ 6. The implied main idea of the second section of the passage entitled "Emotional Arousal" is stated in which sentence?
   a. Emotional arousal occurs in three stages.
   b. Three expert views of emotional arousal offer differing opinions about the number and sequence of the stages of emotional arousal.
   c. One theory places the physiological arousal before the experience of emotion.
   d. Emotions have a physical effect on the individual.

_____ 7. The implied central idea of the entire passage is stated in which sentence?
   a. Emotions cannot be controlled nor fully understood.
   b. The eight basic emotions occur in distinct stages.
   c. Experts have developed theories that help us understand the complexity of human emotions and the process of emotional arousal
   d. Experts in the field disagree about the nature of human emotions.

B. Directions: Use the information in the text and refer to Figure 7.2 to answer the following questions.

_____ 8. The sequence of emotions labeled (a) in the graphic depicts _____.
   a. the James-Lange sequence of emotions
   b. the common-sense view of emotions
   c. the cognitive labeling theory of emotions
   d. the experience of the emotion

_____ 9. The sequence of emotions labeled (b) in the graphic depicts _____.
   a. the experience of the emotion
   b. the cognitive labeling theory of emotions
   c. the common-sense view of emotions
   d. the James-Lange sequence of emotions

_____ 10. The sequence of emotions labeled (c) in the graphic depicts _____.
   a. the James-Lange sequence of emotions
   b. the cognitive labeling theory of emotions
   c. the common-sense view of emotions
   d. the experience of the emotion

Chapter 5: Supporting Details, Outlines, and Concept Maps
LAB 5.1 PRACTICE EXERCISE 1

Name_____Section_____Date_____Score (number correct)_____ x 10 = _____

Objective: To determine the major and minor details that support a topic and the main idea.

Directions: Read following passage and answer the questions that follow.

The Bodacious Boidae Family

[1]Boa is the common name for the Boidae family of snakes, which is made up of 50 species. [2]The best known boa is the boa constrictor, which has been known to grow to over 18 feet long. [3]One of the largest of the boas is the anaconda, which can grow up to 25 feet in length and 3 feet in thickness. [4]The anaconda lives in swamps and the shallow parts of rivers in South America, preying on animals as they come to drink. [5]The python, which is also a nonvenomous constrictor, is another noteworthy member of the Boidae family. [6]Like boas, the muscular python squeezes its prey to death, and it possesses the same hind limbs with claws reminiscent of its lizard ancestry. [7]However, unlike the boa constrictors, the python reproduces by laying eggs around which the female coils herself for the six- to eight-week incubation period. [8]The reticulated python of Southeast Asia is one of the world's largest snakes, reaching lengths of over 30 feet and weighing as much as 300 pounds. [9]The snakes within the Boidae family are remarkable for their variety, strength, and size.

_____ 1. The topic of this paragraph is _____.
    a. snakes
    b. snakes in the Boidae family
    c. venomous snakes
    d. constrictors

_____ 2. The main idea of this paragraph is expressed in _____.
    a. sentence 1
    b. sentence 2
    c. sentence 3
    d. sentence 9

_____ 3. How many major supporting details are in the paragraph?
    a. 1
    b. 2
    c. 3
    d. 4

_____ 4.   Sentence 2 serves as a _____ for the paragraph.
    a. thesis statement
    b. main idea
    c. major supporting detail
    d. minor supporting detail

_____ 5. Sentence 3 serves as a _____ for the paragraph.
   a. main idea
   b. central theme
   c. major supporting detail
   d. minor supporting detail

_____ 6. Sentence 4 serves as a _____ for the paragraph.
   a. main idea
   b. central theme
   c. major supporting detail
   d. minor supporting detail

_____ 7. Sentence 5 serves as a _____ for the paragraph.
   a. main idea
   b. central theme
   c. major supporting detail
   d. minor supporting detail

_____ 8. Sentence 6 serves as a _____ for the paragraph.
   a. main idea
   b. central theme
   c. major supporting detail
   d. minor supporting detail

_____ 9. Sentence 7 serves as a _____ for the paragraph.
   a. main idea
   b. central theme
   c. major supporting detail
   d. minor supporting detail

_____ 10. Which of the following outlines correctly depicts the major details in this paragraph?
   a.
         A. boa constrictor
         B. anaconda
         C. python
         D. reticulatd python

   b.
         A. 18 feet
         B. 25 feet
         C. lives in swamps
         D. lays eggs

   c.
         A. South American snakes
         B.   Southeast Asian snake

   d.
         A. venomous snakes
         B. nonvenomous snake

Chapter 5: Supporting Details, Outlines, and Concept Maps
LAB 5.2 PRACTICE EXERCISE 2

Name_____ Section _____ Date _____ Score (number correct) _____ x 10 = _____

Objective: To identify the topic, main idea, and supporting major and minor details in a textbook passage.

Directions: Read following passage from a sociology textbook, and answer the questions that follow.

[1]The term *morphology* refers to the body's external appearance. [2]Research on the possible relationship between three extreme body types and criminality first began to appear in the early decades of the twentieth century. [3]First, **endomorphy** refers to persons who are extremely rotund (fat) and nonmuscular. [4]Second, **mesomorphy** refers to persons who are unusually muscular in their body build, and to date, all studies have reported significant tendencies for delinquents and criminals to be more mesomorphic than persons in general. [5]The third body type, **ectomorphy,** denotes persons who are very skinny and nonmuscular. [6]Many college students in these studies tend to be more ectomorphic than the general adult population. [7]Finally, in the middle of these three extremes, are persons who are said to have a **balanced body type,** which includes the majority of people. [8]To illustrate the types of findings that have been consistently reported, one of the most famous body type studies found that, whereas 31 percent of nondelinquents were mesmorphic, 60 percent of the delinquents were.

— Adapted from Ellis and Walsh, *Criminology*, p. 278.

_____ 1. The topic of this passage is _____.
  a. body types of delinquents and criminals
  b. body types of college students
  c. most common body types
  d. the relationship between morphology and criminality

_____ 2. The main idea of the paragraph is expressed in _____.
  a. sentence 1
  b. sentence 2
  c. sentence 3
  d. sentence 4

_____ 3. Sentence 3 serves as a _____ for the paragraph.
  a. thesis statement
  b. main idea
  c. summary statement
  d. major supporting detail

_____ 4. Sentence 4 serves as a _____ for the paragraph.
  a. main idea
  b. major supporting detail
  c. minor supporting detail
  d. summary statement

71

_____ 5. Sentence 5 serves as a _____ for the paragraph.
   a. thesis statement
   b. main idea
   c. major supporting detail
   d. minor supporting detail

_____ 6. Sentence 6 serves as a _____ for the paragraph.
   a. main idea
   b. major supporting detail
   c. minor supporting detail
   d. summary statement

_____ 7. Sentence 7 serves as a _____ for the paragraph.
   a. thesis statement
   b. main idea
   c. major supporting detail
   d. minor supporting detail

_____ 8. Sentence 8 serves as a _____ for the paragraph.
   a. main idea
   b. major supporting detail
   c. minor supporting detail
   d. summary statement

_____ 9. According to the selection, ectomorphs include more _____ than the general population.
   a. juvenile delinquents
   b. criminals
   c. athletes
   d. college students

_____ 10. The term *morphology* refers to _____.
   a. the body's external appearances
   b. the relationship between body types and criminality
   c. ways in which scientists track delinquency
   d. ways in which men are encouraged to change their body type

Chapter 5: Supporting Details, Outlines, and Concept Maps
LAB 5.3 REVIEW TEST 1

Name_____ Section _____ Date _____ Score (number correct) _____ x 10 = _____

Directions: Read following the following passage and then answer the questions that follow.

Restrictions on the Media

[1]Powerful as they are in social and cultural influence, the mass media in turn are restricted in numerous ways by other segments of society. [2]Editors and producers are limited in what they present to the public by laws concerning libel, invasion of privacy, copyright, and pornography. [3]Equally strong, and in some ways more restrictive, are pressures from special-interest groups, and difficulty in meeting loosely defined standards of good taste.

[4]One major restriction comes from activists. [5]Using threats of boycotts to harm the supposedly offending media financially, activists for causes demand that editors delete story material and phraseology they dislike. [6]They also demand publication of stories favorable to them. [7]They cry "biased reporting" if the editors reject their demands.

[8]Pressure on the media comes from other sources as well. [9]Among the strongest pressures are those from the "religious right." [10]Conservative religious groups campaign against motion pictures and television shows whose content fails to conform to their strict standards of behavior and language.

[11]Minority groups offer their own form of pressure. [12]Various minority groups detect what they regard as racial slurs in public utterances and news coverage. [13]Some newspapers have been pressured into apologizing publicly for editorial cartoons regarded as racist by activist organizations.

[14]Even advertisers are guilty of placing pressure on the media, though on a different level. [15]Commercial retaliation by advertisers displeased by stories they consider harmful to their businesses, while relatively rare, sometimes results in cancellation of advertising contracts as punishment. [16]Public officials and local booster groups also seek revenge for unfavorable coverage by urging citizens to cancel subscriptions or refuse to watch a certain television show.

[17]In sum, then, the mass media strongly influence public opinion and behavior, but public opinion in turn exercises substantial, if not always obvious, restraint on the media.

— Adapted from Agee, Ault, and Emery, *Introduction to Mass Communications*, 12th ed., pp. 26–28.

_____ 1. The topic of this passage is _____.
   a. the growing number of complaints against the media
   b. the number of boycotts from advertisers
   c. restrictions on the media
   d. conservative religious groups

_____ 2. The central idea of the passage is stated in _____.
   a. sentence 2
   b. sentence 3
   c. sentence 5
   d. sentence 17

_____ 3. The main idea of the second paragraph is stated in _____.
   a. sentence 4
   b. sentence 5
   c. sentence 6
   d. sentence 7

_____ 4. Sentence 5 is _____.
   a. a central idea
   b. a main idea
   c. a major supporting detail
   d. a minor supporting detail

_____ 5. Sentence 6 is _____.
   a. a central idea
   b. a main idea
   c. a major supporting
   d. a minor supporting detail

_____ 6. Sentence 7 is _____.
   a. a central idea
   b. a main idea
   c. a major supporting
   d. a detail minor supporting detail

_____ 7. Sentence 8 is _____.
   a. a central idea
   b. a main idea
   c. a major supporting
   d. a minor supporting detail

_____ 8. Sentence 11 is _____.
   a. a central idea
   b. a main idea
   c. a major supporting
   d. a detail minor supporting detail

_____ 9. Sentence 12 is _____.
   a. a central idea
   b. a main idea
   c. a major supporting
   d. a minor supporting detail

_____ 10. Sentence 14 is _____.
   a. a central idea
   b. a main idea
   c. a major supporting
   d. a minor supporting detail

Chapter 5: Supporting Details, Outlines, and Concept Maps
LAB 5.4 REVIEW TEST 2

Name_____ Section _____ Date _____ Score (number correct) _____ x 10 = _____

Directions: Read the paragraph and study the main idea presented. Then answer the questions that follow.

[1]Humanity has devised many ways to harness the renewable and nonrenewable forms of energy available on our planet. [2]We use these energy sources to heat and light our homes, power our machinery, fuel our vehicles, and provide the comforts and conveniences to which we've grown accustomed in the industrial age. [3]In order to obtain the energy we need to sustain this lifestyle, we use a variety of sources, some renewable and some nonrenewable.

[4]Renewable sources of energy will not be depleted by our use. [5]One kind of renewable energy is geo-thermal power. [6]This energy emanates from Earth's core, enabling us to harness it. [7]A second source of energy is nuclear power. [8]This is the great deal of energy that resides within bonds among protons and neutron in atoms. [9]The gravitational pull of the moon and sun generate another much smaller amount of energy, tidal power. [10]We are just beginning to harness this energy from the ocean tides as a result of the gravitational pull of the moon and sun. [11]Most of Earth's energy, however, comes from the sun. [12]Solar radiation helps drive wind patterns and the hydrologic cycle, making possible forms of energy such as wind power and hydroelectric power. [13]And of course, sunlight drives the growth of plants, from which we take wood and other biomass as a fuel source. [14]Finally, when plants die, some may impart their stored chemical energy to fossil fuels, highly combustible substances formed from the remains of organisms from past geological ages.

—Adapted from Withgott and Brennan, *Essential Environment: The Science Behind the Stories*, 3rd ed., pp. 329-330.

_____ 1. The topic of this passage is _____.
a. sustaining our lifestyle
b. sources of energy
c. sources of renewable energy
d. sources of nonrenewable energy

_____ 2. The controlling idea of the passage is expressed in _____.
a. sentence 1
b. sentence 2
c. sentence 3
d. sentence 4

_____ 3. Which sentence states the main idea in the second paragraph?
a. sentence 4
b. sentence 5
c. sentence 6
d. sentence 14

_____ 4. Sentence 5 serves as a _____ for the second paragraph.
   a. topic
   b. main idea sentence
   c. major supporting detail
   d. minor supporting detail

_____ 5. Sentence 6 serves as a _____ for the second paragraph.
   a. topic
   b. main idea sentence
   c. major supporting detail
   d. minor supporting detail

_____ 6. Sentence 7 serves as a _____ for the second paragraph.
   a. topic
   b. main idea sentence
   c. major supporting detail
   d. minor supporting detail

_____ 7. The words *for example* in sentence 12 indicate that this sentence serves as a _____ for the paragraph.
   a. topic
   b. main idea
   c. supporting detail
   d. central idea

_____ 8. Sentence 14 serves as a _____ for the second paragraph.
   a. topic
   b. main idea sentence
   c. major supporting detail
   d. minor supporting detail

Directions: Choose the major details that will complete this concept map.

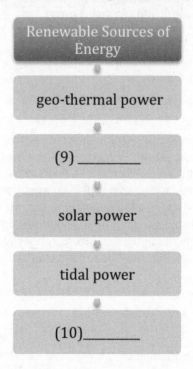

_____ 9. The best choice for number 9 on the concept map is _____ .
    a. nuclear power
    b. protons
    c. neutrons
    d. energy power

_____ 10. The best choice for number 10 on the concept map is _____ ..
    a. biomass fuels
    b. hydroelectric power
    c. wind power
    d. solar energy

Chapter 5: Supporting Details, Outlines, and Concept Maps
LAB 5.5 MASTERY TEST 1

Name_____ Section _____ Date _____ Score (number correct) _____ x 10 = _____

Directions: Read the paragraphs, and answer the questions that follow.

A. [1]Arguments about how to teach mathematics resemble those in reading. [2]Drill in computational skills is pitted against "number sense," or understanding. [3]Yet once again, a blend of these two approaches is most beneficial. [4]In learning math facts, poorly performing students spend little time experimenting with strategies but, instead, move quickly toward trying to retrieve answers from memory. [5]Their responses are often wrong because they have not used strategies long enough to test which ones result in rapid, accurate solutions. [6]By trying out strategies, good students grapple with underlying concepts and develop effective solution techniques. [7]This suggests that encouraging students to apply strategies and making sure they understand why certain strategies work well are vital for solid mastery of basic math.

—Berk, *Development Through the Lifespan*, 3rd ed., p. 292.

_____ 1. The topic of this paragraph is _____.
   a. arguments about teaching mathematics
   b. best strategies for learning math
   c. poor math students
   d. good math students

_____ 2. Sentence 3 serves as a _____ for the paragraph.
   a. main idea
   b. major supporting detail
   c. minor supporting detail
   d. central idea

_____ 3. Sentence 4 serves as a _____ for the paragraph.
   a. main idea
   b. major supporting detail
   c. minor supporting detail
   d. topic

_____ 4. Sentence 5 serves as a _____ for the paragraph.
   a. main idea
   b. major supporting detail
   c. minor supporting detail
   d. summarizing sentence

_____ 5. Sentence 6 serves as a _____ for the paragraph.
   a. main idea
   b. major supporting detail
   c. minor supporting detail
   d. concluding sentence

____ 6. Sentence 7 _____.
   a. restates the main idea
   b. serves as a major supporting detail
   c. serves as a minor supporting detail
   d. is a concluding sentence

B. [1]Think of the recent excuses you have used or heard. [2]Did they fall into any of these three classes? [3]The first is "I didn't do it." [4]Here you deny that you have done what you're being accused of doing. [5]You might then bring up an alibi to prove you couldn't have done it, or perhaps you might accuse another person of doing that for which you are being blamed. [6]("I never said that" or "I wasn't even near the place when it happened.") [7]The second class of excuse is "It wasn't so bad." [8]Here you admit to doing it, but claim the offense was not really so bad or perhaps that there was justification for the behavior. [9]("I only padded the expense account and even then only modestly" or "Sure, I hit him, but he was asking for it.") [10]The final class of excuse is "Yes, but." [11]Here you claim that extenuating circumstances accounted for the behavior, for example, you weren't in control at the time or you didn't intend to do what you did. [12]("It was the liquor talking" or "I never intended to hurt him. I was actually trying to help.")

—Adapted from DeVito, *The Interpersonal Communication Book*, 10th ed., pp. 229–230.

____ 7. The topic of this paragraph is _____.
   a. poor behavior
   b. justification for behavior
   c. etiquette rules
   d. types of excuses

____ 8. Sentence 1 serves as a _____ for the paragraph.
   a. main idea
   b. major supporting detail
   c. minor supporting detail
   d. central idea

____ 9. Sentence 4 serves as a _____ for the paragraph.
   a. main idea
   b. major supporting detail
   c. minor supporting detail
   d. topic

___ 10. This paragraph contains _____ major details.
   a. 2
   b. 3
   c. 4
   d. 5

Name _____ Section _____ Date _____ Score (number correct) _____ x 10 = _____

Directions: Read the passage, and answer the questions that follow.

[1]Maintainig a nutritious diet within the confines of student life can be challenging. [2]However, if you take the time to plan healthy meals, you will find that you are eating better, enjoying your food more, and actually saving money. [3]Follow these steps to ensure a healthy but affordable diet at home.

[4]Buy fruits and vegetables in season whenever possible for their lower cost, higher nutrient quality, and greater variety. [5]Wash all produce, even bagged items, before eating. [6]Don't bother buying veggie washes and other products. [7]A fast-flowing water faucet, brisk rubbing with your hands, soaking in salt water, or other cleaning techniques are more effective and cost less.

[8]Buy locally, whenever possible. [9]Fresh produce is often higher in nutrients and, if organic, has fewer pesticides and other chemicals. [10]By purchasing imported fresh fruits and vegetables, you are putting yourself at risk for ingesting exotic pathogens or even pesticides that have been banned in the United States for safety reasons. [11]For example, up to 70 percent of the fruits and vegetables consumed in the United States come from Mexico alone.

[12]Planning is another way to keep food costs within reason. [13]Use coupons and specials to get price reductions. [14]Plan your menu for the week, make a list, and stick to it so you can avoid impulse shopping. [15]No food is cheap if you don't eat it.

[16]Shop at discount warehouse food chains; capitalize on volume discounts and no-frills products. [17]However, don't buy more than you can reasonable use before "shelf life" expirations.

[18]Finally, when time is short, eat healthily while eating out. [19]At least once per week, substitute a vegetable-based meat substitute into your fast-food choices. [20]Most places now offer Gardenburgers, Boca burgers, and similar products, which provide excellent sources of protein and often have considerably less fat and fewer calories.

—Adapted from Donatelle, *Health: the Basics*, 8th ed., pp. 278–279.

_____ 1. The topic of this passage is _____.
   a. the challenges of student life
   b. the dangers of imported foods
   c. using coupons
   d. ensuring a health and affordable diet

_____ 2. The controlling idea of the passage is expressed in _____.
   a. sentence 1
   b. sentence 2
   c. sentence 8
   d. sentence 18

_____ 3. Which sentence states the main idea in the second paragraph?
   a. sentence 4
   b. sentence 5
   c. sentence 6
   d. sentence 7

_____ 4. Sentence 5 serves as a _____ for the second paragraph.
   a. topic
   b. main idea sentence
   c. major supporting detail
   d. minor supporting detail

_____ 5. Sentence 7 serves as a _____ for the second paragraph.
   a. topic
   b. main idea sentence
   c. major supporting detail
   d. minor supporting detail

_____ 6. Sentence 8 serves as a _____ for the second paragraph.
   a. topic
   b. main idea sentence
   c. major supporting detail
   d. minor supporting detail

_____ 7. The words *for example* in sentence 11 indicate that this sentence serves as a _____ for the paragraph.
   a. topic
   b. main idea
   c. supporting detail
   d. central idea

_____ 8. Sentence 13 serves as a _____ for the second paragraph.
   a. topic
   b. main idea sentence
   c. major supporting detail
   d. minor supporting detail

_____ 9. Sentence 15 serves as a _____ for the second paragraph.
   a. topic
   b. main idea sentence
   c. major supporting detail
   d. minor supporting detail

_____ 10. Sentence 19 serves as a _____ for the second paragraph.
   a. topic
   b. main idea sentence
   c. major supporting detail
   d. minor supporting detail

Name _____ Section _____ Date _____ Score (number correct) _____ x 10 = _____

Objective: To outline major and minor details that support the central idea.

Directions: Read the paragraphs and answer the questions that follow.

[1]Children's long-term adjustment depends on the **goodness-of-fit** of their particular temperament with the nature and demands of the environment in which they find themselves. [2]For instance, children with a low activity level and low irritability may do particularly well in an environment in which they are left to explore on their own and are allowed largely to direct their own behavior. [3]In contrast, high-activity-level, highly irritable children may do best with greater direction. [4]This will permit them to channel their energy in a particular direction. [5]To use this knowledge effectively, parents can then find ways to adjust the environment for their own children. [6]For example, if parents react to difficult behavior by showing anger and inconsistency, then the child is ultimately more likely to experience behavior problems. [7]On the other hand, parents who display more warmth and consistency in their responses are more likely to have a child who avoids later problems.

—Adapted from Feldman, *Child Development*, 5th ed., p. 175.

_____1. The main idea of the passage is stated in _____.
  a. sentence 1
  b. sentence 2
  c. sentence 3
  d. sentence 4

_____2. In general, the main idea is supported by _____.
  a. characteristics of temperament
  b. a list of arguments opposing theories of temperament
  c. examples of opposing temperaments and parental behaviors
  d. facts about good parenting skills

_____3. Sentence 2 serves as a _____ for the passage.
  a. the topic of the entire passage
  b. the central idea of the entire passage
  c. a major detail supporting the main idea
  d. a minor detail supporting the first major point

_____4. How many supporting details provide different examples of goodness-of-fit?
  a. two
  b. three
  c. four
  d. five

_____5. How many supporting details provide examples of parenting behaviors?
  a. one
  b. two
  c. three
  d. four

82

_____6. The words that introduce the details in support of goodness-of-fit are _____.
   a. long-term adjustment
   b. demands of the environment
   c. this will permit
   d. for instance, in contrast

_____7. The words that introduce the details in support of parenting behavior are_____.
   a. to use this
   b. parents can then
   c. for example, on the other hand
   d. low activity level, high-activity-level

8–10. Fill in the outline by completing the heading and filling in the two major details that are missing.

Goodness-of-fit affects (8)_____.

   1. (9) Activity and _____ levels can be matched with types of environment.

   2. (10)_____ can adjust the environment of their own children.

   3. Parent's reactions to difficult behavior affect children in later years.

Name_____ Section _____ Date _____ Score (number correct) _____ x 10 = _____

Objective: To map the major and minor details supporting a central idea.

Directions: Fill in the concept map with supporting details from the list in a logical order that supports the central idea.

Paragraph A

A legend found in Mexico as well as Central and South America is that of La Llorona (the Weeping Woman). So fascinating did she become in the oral tradition of passing stories from one generation to the next that numerous versions of her persist. In one she is a phantom woman, never seen, but heard weeping in the night. She is supposedly mourning her children, for whose deaths she is responsible. In another tale she is a spirit doomed to wander forever in search of the children she neglected during her lifetime. Still another story shows her to be blatantly evil, someone who lures men into following her, only to meet up with violent death at her hands. This character is similar to the Sirens in Greek mythology, the sea maidens whose singing is so seductive that ships sail toward them, but are dashed to pieces on the rocks. It also forms the basis for the enduring German folk song "Die Lorelei," about a beautiful maiden who sits on a rock, combing her hair and singing so beautifully that, again, ships are wrecked and many lives are lost.

The tales of La Llorona are often told as a warning to young unmarried pregnant women who find themselves abandoned and have no recourse but to give up their babies. Presumably, repeating the story of a mother mourning her lost children reminds young women of what can happen when they indulge in practices forbidden by religion and family.

— Janaro and Altshuler, *The Art of Being Human,* 7th ed., pp. 84–85.

_____ 1. The best heading for a concept map of this passage is _____.
   a. Tales of La Llorona (the Weeping Woman)
   b. Legends of Mexico
   c. Oral traditions
   d. Greek Mythology

_____ 2. The major details in this paragraph are intended to _____.
   a. explain the reasons for oral history
   b. describe the pattern of oral traditions in Mexico
   c. analyze the reasons for legends that persist in Mexico
   d. list the three versions about La Llorona

3–5. Insert the details that support the central idea in the concept map below.

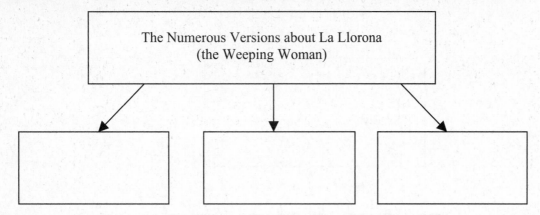

Paragraph B

[1]The earliest known terrorist group was a Jewish nationalist/religious group called the *Sicarii.* [2]They operated against occupying Roman forces around 70 A.D. using deadly savage methods against Romans and Jews alike. [3]Another early group, the *Ismailis* or *Assassins*, responding to what they considered religious oppression, carried out a reign of intimidation throughout the Islamic world from about the eleventh to the mid-thirteenth centuries, and have been called the most effective terrorists in history. [4]The term *terrorism* itself is believed to have originated with the French Revolutionary Jacobins who instituted France's domestic Reign of Terror. [5]Thus, the phenomenon of terrorism is neither new nor alien to human nature.

— Adapted from Ellis and Walsh, *Criminology,* 2000, p. 502.

_____ 6.   Sentence 1 serves as a _____.
   a.   main idea for paragraph B
   b.   major detail supporting the main idea for the paragraph
   c.   minor detail supporting a major detail for the paragraph
   d.   central idea of the passage

_____ 7.   Sentence 5 serves as a _____.
   a.   main idea for the paragraph
   b.   major detail supporting the main idea for the paragraph
   c.   minor detail supporting a major detail for the paragraph
   d.   a connection to the next paragraph

8–10. Complete the concept map by filling in the blanks.

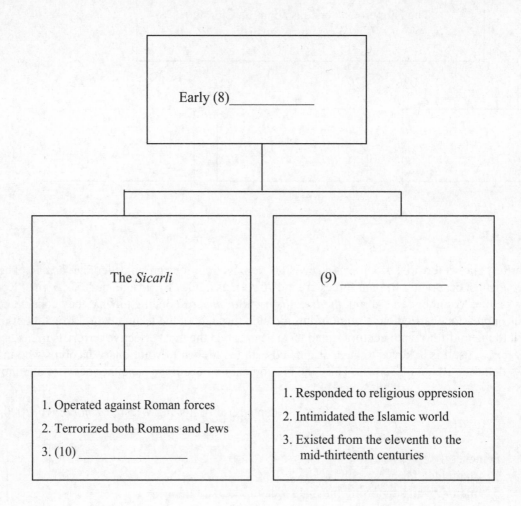

Early (8)_____

The *Sicarli*

(9)_____

1. Operated against Roman forces

2. Terrorized both Romans and Jews

3. (10) _____

1. Responded to religious oppression

2. Intimidated the Islamic world

3. Existed from the eleventh to the mid-thirteenth centuries

Chapter 6: Outlines and Concept Maps
LAB 6.3 REVIEW TEST 1

Name_____ Section _____ Date _____ Score (number correct) _____ x 10 = _____

Objective: To outline major and minor details that support the central idea.

Directions: Read the paragraphs and answer the questions that follow.

[1]Do you accept the cliché that one person's terrorist is another's freedom fighter? [2]Although many people do, this attitude has been called "sophomoric moral relativism." [3]Although all terrorists probably claim to be freedom fighters, there are two important distinctions between terrorists and freedom fighters (or guerrillas) that go beyond semantics implying their moral equivalence. [4]First, freedom fighters are fighters in wars of national liberation against foreign occupiers or against oppressive domestic regimes they seek to overthrow. [5]Terrorists are typically fighting to gain some sort of ethnic autonomy or to right some perceived inequity and rarely have illusions of overthrowing the government they are fighting against. [6]While guerrillas may occasionally use terrorist tactics against noncombatants, widespread use of such tactics will deprive them of the popular support they need, and thus they tend to confine their activities to fighting enemy combatants.

[7]The second important distinction is that guerrilla activity is overwhelmingly confined to third-world dictatorships or one-party states, while terrorists overwhelmingly operate against liberal Western democracies, which are less well-equipped to deal with the problem because of legal and moral restraints than are ruthless dictatorships or one-party states.

— Ellis and Walsh, *Criminology,* 2000, p. 503.

_____ 1.   The topic of this passage is _____.
   a.   sophomoric moral relativism
   b.   terrorism
   c.   guerilla activity
   d.   distinctions between terrorists and freedom fighters

_____ 2.   The central idea of the passage is stated in _____.
   a.   sentence 1
   b.   sentence 2
   c.   sentence 3
   d.   sentence 6

_____ 3.   The major points of this passage will most likely explain _____.
   a.   how to become a freedom fighter
   b.   how to succeed in overcoming third-world dictatorships
   c.   the terms used by psychologists who study terrorism
   d.   the difference between terrorists and freedom fighters

_____ 4. Sentence 4 serves as a _____ for the passage.
   a. central theme
   b. topic
   c. major detail for the passage
   d. minor supporting detail for a major detail

_____ 5. How many major points support the central idea of this passage?
   a. one
   b. two
   c. three
   d. four

6–10. Fill in the outline by completing the major and minor details that are missing.

Differences between Terrorists and Freedom Fighters

1. Freedom fighters (guerillas) fight (6) _____.

   a. They seek to overthrow the government.

   b. (7)_____.

   c. They limit activities to the enemy.

   d. Their activity is confined (8)_____.

2. Terrorists fight (9) to gain ethnic autonomy or to right some perceived inequity.

   a. They rarely have illusions of overthrowing governments.

   b. (10)_____.

Name _____ Section _____ Date _____ Score (number correct) _____ x 10 = _____

Directions: Read the paragraphs and answer the questions that follow.

[1]Exercising or performing manual labor in extreme heat and humidity is very dangerous for two reasons. [2]First of all, the extreme heat dramatically raises body temperature. [3]During intense activity in the heat, our muscles and skin are constantly competing for blood flow. [4]When there is no longer enough blood flow to simultaneously provide adequate blood to our muscles and to our skin, muscle blood flow takes priority over the skin, which prevents us from cooling ourselves. [5]The second reason extreme heat and humidity can be dangerous is that high humidity prohibits evaporative cooling. [6]During periods of high humidity, the environmental air is so saturated with water that it is unable to pull water from the surface of the skin. [7]Under both of these conditions, heat illnesses are likely to occur, and they include several types:

- [8]**Heat syncope** is dizziness that occurs when people stand too long in the heat, and the blood pools n their lower extremities. [9]It can also occur when people stop suddenly after a race or stand suddenly from a lying position.
- [10]**Heat cramps** are muscle spasms that can occur during exercise or several hours after strenuous exercise or manual labor. [11]They are most commonly felt in the legs, arms, or abdomen after a person cools down. [12]They occur during times when sweat losses and fluid intakes are high, urine volume is low, and sodium intake is inadequate to replace losses.
- [13]**Heat exhaustion** and **heatstroke** occur on a continuum, with unchecked heat exhaustion leading to heatstroke. [14]Early signs of heat exhaustion include excessive sweating, cold and clammy skin, rapid but weak pulse, weakness, nausea, dizziness, headache, and difficulty concentrating. [15]As this condition progresses, consciousness becomes impaired. [16]Prompt medical care is essential to save the person's life.

—Adapted from Thompson and Manore, *Nutrition for Life*, 2nd ed., pp.322–323.

_____1. The topic this passage is
   a. exercising
   b. manual labor
   c. heat-related problems and illnesses
   d. characteristics of exercising programs

_____2. The central idea of the passage is stated in _____.
   a. sentence 1
   b. sentence 2
   c. sentence 3
   d. sentence 6

_____3. The major points of this passage explain _____.
   a. how to avoid heat-related illnesses
   b. how to overcome heat-related illnesses
   c. the terms and definitions used to discuss heat related illnesses
   d. the importance of exercising even during periods of intense heat

_____4. Sentence 5 serves as a _____ for the passage.
    a. central theme
    b. topic
    c. major detail for the passage
    d. minor supporting detail for a major detail

_____5. How many major points support the main idea of the first paragraph?
    a. one
    b. two
    c. three
    d. four

6-10. Fill in the outline by completing the major and minor details that are missing.

Causes and Types of Heat-Related Illnesses

1. Extreme heat dramatically (6) _____

    a. Muscles and skin compete for blood flow.

    b. If there isn't enough blood flow, (7)_____

2. High humidity (8) _____

3. Types of _____

    a. Heat syncope

    b. _____

    c. Heat exhaustion

    d. Heat stroke

Name_____Section _____ Date _____Score (number correct) _____ x 10 = _____

Directions: Read the paragraphs and answer the questions that follow.

Paragraph A

[1]Just about everything is arguable, but much of the time certain types of argument are not advanced. [2]For one, statements of **fact** are usually not considered arguable. [3]Jeff's claim that students at universities in the United Kingdom do not pay tuition is a statement of fact that turned out not to be true. [4]Most facts can be verified by doing research. But even simple facts can sometimes be argued. [5]For example, Mount Everest is usually acknowledged to be the highest mountain in the world at 29,028 feet above sea level. [6]But if the total height of a mountain from base to summit is the measure, then the volcano Mauna Loa in Hawaii is the highest mountain in the world. [7]Although the top of Mauna Loa is 13,667 feet above sea level, the summit is 31,784 feet above the ocean floor. [8]Thus the "fact" that Mount Everest is the highest mountain on the earth depends on a definition of *highest* being the point farthest above sea level. [9]You could argue for this definition.

[10]Another category of claims that are not arguable are those of **personal taste.** [11]Your favorite food and your favorite color are examples of personal taste. [12]If you hate fresh tomatoes, no one can convince you that you actually like them. [13]But many claims of personal taste turn out to be value judgments using arguable criteria. [14]For instance, if you think that *Alien* is the best science fiction movie ever made, you can argue that claim using evaluative criteria that other people can consider as good reasons. [15]Indeed, you might not even like science fiction and still argue that *Alien* is the best science fiction movie ever.

[16]Finally, many claims rest on **beliefs** or **faith**. [17]If someone accepts a claim as a matter of religious belief, then for that person, the claim is true and cannot be refuted. [18]Of course, people still make arguments about the existence of God and which religion reflects the will of God. [19]Any time an audience will not consider an idea, it's possible but very difficult to construct an argument. [20]Many people claim that UFOs exist, but most people refuse to acknowledge that evidence as even being possibly factual.

— Adapted from Faigley and Selzer, *Good Reasons,* 2nd ed., p. 32–33.

_____ 1. The topic of this passage is _____.
   a. statement of fact
   b. statements of personal taste
   c. inarguable claims
   d. beliefs of faith

_____ 2. The central idea of the passage is stated in _____.
   a. sentence 1
   b. sentence 8
   c. sentence 10
   d. sentence 16

_____ 3. The major points of this passage are intended to be _____.
   a. explain why people argue so much
   b. provide examples of arguments
   c. list the types of claims that are not usually arguable
   d. describe the arguments constructed against religion

_____ 4. Sentence 5 serves as a _____ for the paragraph.
   a. main idea
   b. major supporting detail
   c. minor supporting detail
   d. specific example

_____ 5. Which words in the passage signal the major supporting details?
   a. *much of the time*
   b. *for one, another category,* and *finally*
   c. *for example, examples,* and *for instance*
   d. *but* and *if*

_____ 6. The main idea of paragraph 2 is stated in _____ .
   a. sentence 10
   b. sentence 12
   c. sentence 13
   d. sentence 15

_____ 7. Sentence 11 serves as a _____ for the paragraph.
   a. main idea
   b. major supporting detail
   c. minor supporting detail
   d. specific example

8–10. Fill in the outline by completing the major and minor details that are missing.

Inarguable Claims

1. (8) _____.

2. (9) _____.

   a. Favorite foods and favorite colors are examples.

   b. Many claims of personal taste turn out to be value judgments using arguable criteria.

3. Statement of belief or faith.

   a. (10)_____.

   b. Most people refuse to acknowledge that evidence is factual for claims of the existence of UFOs.

Chapter 6: Outlines and Concept Maps
LAB 6.6 MASTERY TEST 2

Name_____ Section _____ Date _____ Score (number correct) _____ x 10 = _____

Directions: Read the paragraph and answer the questions that follow.

[1]Literature operates through a system of language in which the words themselves trigger our understanding. [2]Like many other arts, we approach literature through the formal door of its genres. [3]Literature can be divided into four types.

[4]Fiction is a work created from the author's imagination rather than from fact. [5]Normally, it takes one of two approaches to its subject matter. [6]Fiction is either realistic and uses observable, true-to-life details, or it is nonrealistic and explores fantasy. [7]Other literary forms, such as narrative poetry, however, can also be fiction. [8]Traits of fiction can be used in other forms such as biography and epic poetry. [9]By tradition, fiction is divided into novels and short stories.

[10]Poetry, on the other hand, is a type of work designed to convey a vivid and imaginative sense of experience. [11]It uses concentrated language, selected for its sound, suggestive power, and meaning. [12]In addition, it uses specific devices such as meter, rhyme, and metaphor. [13]Poetry can be divided into three major types: narrative, which tells a story; dramatic, which uses dramatic form; and lyric, which expresses the personal emotion of the poet.

[14]Over the centuries, biography, a written account of a person's life, has taken many forms. [15]Some of these include literary narratives, simple catalogues of achievement, and psychological portraits.

[16]The essay is a short literary composition on a single subject, usually presenting the personal views of the author. [17]Essays include many subforms and a variety of styles, but they uniformly present a personal point of view with a deliberate attempt to achieve grace of expression. [18]The best essays are marked by clarity, good humor, and tolerance.

— Adapted from Sporre, *The Creative Impulse,* 6th ed., p. 22.

_____ 1. Sentence 3 is a _____.
   a. thesis statement
   b. main idea
   c. major supporting detail
   d. minor supporting detail

_____ 2. How many major supporting details are in this passage?
   a. 2
   b. 3
   c. 4
   d. 5

_____ 3. What word or phrase introduces the second major supporting detail?
   a. *normally*
   b. *by tradition*
   c. *and*
   d. *on the other hand*

_____ 4. In the fifth paragraph (sentences 16-18), sentence 16 is _____.
   a. the main idea
   b. a major supporting detail
   c. a minor supporting detail
   d. a specific example

_____ 5. In general, the supporting details of the second paragraph _____.
   a. explain the differences between fiction and poetry
   b. explain some of the traits of fiction
   c. argue that fiction is the best type of literature
   d. give examples of great works of fiction

8–10. Complete the concept map with the main idea and major supporting details from the passage.

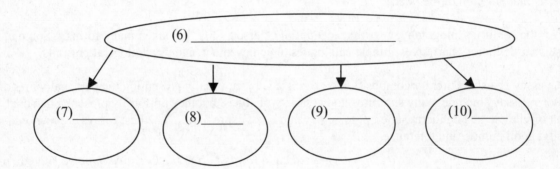

(6) _____

(7)_____   (8)_____   (9)_____   (10)_____

Chapter 7: Transitions and Thought Patterns
LAB 7.1 PRACTICE EXERCISE 1

Name_____ Section _____ Date _____ Score (number correct) _____ x 10 = _____

Objective: To use time and pace order transitions to see the relationship of details to the main idea

A. Directions: Read the paragraphs and insert the appropriate transition from the box on the numbered lines.

and	while	also	between	when

(__1__) 1964 and 1971, nonwhite, and female Americans laid claim to greater equality. The ratification of the Twenty-Sixth Amendment in 1971 reduced the voting age from 21 to 18, in acknowledgment of the sacrifices of young people sent to fight in Vietnam. Women challenged and overcame traditional limits on their personal and work lives. Racial discrimination (__2__) segregation were outlawed. These years (__3__) witnessed striking contradictions. The nation accomplished humanity's age-old dream of walking on the surface of the moon (__4__) Neil Armstrong stepped out of the *Apollo 11* spacecraft on July 20, 1969, (__5__) at home the country sometimes appeared to be coming apart at the seams. Poverty rates dropped to their lowest point ever, yet violence seemed to pervade the land.

> —Adapted from Jones et al., Created Equal: *A History of the United States*, Combined Volume, brief 3rd ed., p. 614.

_____ 6. What thought pattern organizes the sentences as a paragraph?
   a. listing
   b. space order
   c. time order
   d. classification

B. Directions: Select the suitable transition word or expression to complete each sentence. These sentences were adapted from the following college textbook: Thompson and Manore, *Nutrition for Life*, 2nd ed., pp.2-3.

_____ 7. Early nutrition science _____focused on identifying the effect of nutrient deficiencies on human health.
   a. finally
   b. when
   c. then
   d. first

_____ 8. For instance, _____ on long sea voyages, scurvy plagued sailors who had no access to fresh fruits and vegetables and thus consumed no vitamin C.
   a. while
   b. during
   c. prior to
   d. after

_____ 9. The severity of such nutrient-deficiency diseases _____ led nutritionists to establish guidelines for healthy eating such as the Dietary Reference Intakes (DRIs).
   a. during
   b. prior to
   c. when
   d. then

_____ 10. _____ to preventing nutrient-deficiency diseases, a healthful diet can reduce your risk for many of the chronic diseases that are among the top ten causes of death in the United States.
   a. also
   b. while
   c. in addition
   d. previously

Chapter 7: Transitions and Thought Patterns
LAB 7.2 PRACTICE EXERCISE 2

Name_____ Section _____ Date _____ Score (number correct) _____ x 10 = _____

Objective: To use addition transitions and the listing pattern to see the relationship of details to the main idea.

A. Directions: Choose a word from the box to fill in the blanks with transitions that show the relationship between ideas.

when	again	after	during	often

The struggles of blacks for equality went hand in hand with the struggles of those of Mexican descent, principally in the Southwest. (__1__) World War I, thousands of immigrants from Mexico flocked into that part of the country, mingling with the far larger native-born Hispanic population. They could do so legally because the restrictive immigration legislation of the 1920s did not apply to Western Hemisphere nations. (__2__) the Great Depression struck, Mexican Americans were the first to suffer—about half a million Hispanics who were not citizens were either deported or "persuaded" to return to Mexico. But (__3__) World War II and (__4__) between 1948 and 1965, federal legislation encouraged the importation of *braceros* (temporary farm workers). Many other Mexicans entered the country illegally. The latter were known as *mojados*, or "wetbacks," because they (__5__) slipped over the border by swimming across the Rio Grande.

> —Adapted from Carnes and Garraty, *The American Nation*, 11th ed., pp. 827, 830.

B. Directions: Read the paragraph and answer the questions that follow.

[1]The largest features of the continents can be grouped into two distinct categories: extensive, flat, stable areas that have been eroded nearly to sea level, and uplifted regions of deformed rocks that make up present-day mountain belts. [2]The first areas, the stable interiors, have been relatively stable for the last 600 million years or even longer. [3]Typically, these regions were involved in mountain-building episodes much earlier in Earth's history. [4]The second region, the mountain belts, are located principally in two major zones. [5]The circum-Pacific belt (the region surrounding the Pacific Ocean) and the belt that extends eastward from the Alps through Iran and the Himalayas and then dips southward into Indonesia. [6]Older mountains are _____ found on the continents. [7]Examples include the Appalachians in the eastern United States and the Urals in Russia. [8]Their once-lofty peaks are now worn low, the result of millions of years of erosion.

> —Adapted from Tarbuck, Lutgens, and Tasa, *Earth Science*, 12th ed., p. 19.

____ 6. The first major supporting detail is signaled by the transition word _____.
   a. *two*
   b. *distinct*
   c. *first*
   d. *region*

____ 7. The second major supporting detail is signaled by the transition word _____.
   a. *second*
   b. *from*
   c. *another*
   d. *also*

____ 8. The predominant thought pattern used in the paragraph is _____.
   a. listing
   b. time pattern
   c. space order
   d. classification

____ 9. The space pattern is a secondary thought pattern that is indicated by the words _____.
   a. *lofty peaks*
   b. *two distinct groups*
   c. *located, extends, and found*
   d. *millions of years*

___ 10. The transition word that best fits the blank in sentence 6 is _____.
   a. first
   b. often
   c. soon
   d. also

Chapter 7: Transitions and Thought Patterns
LAB 7.3 REVIEW TEST 1

Name_____ Section _____ Date _____ Score (number correct) _____ x 10 = _____

Directions: Read the passages and answer the questions that follow.

Paragraph A

[1]America produced no Galileo or Newton, but colonists contributed significantly to the collection of scientific knowledge. [2]One example is Benjamin Franklin, whose far-ranging curiosity extended to science. [3]"No one of the present age has made more important discoveries," Thomas Jefferson declared. [4]One of Franklin's biographers has similarly called him a "harmonious human multitude." [5]His studies of electricity, which he capped in 1752 with his famous kite experiment, established him as a scientist of international stature. [6]He _____ invented the lightning rod, the iron Franklin stove (a far more efficient way to heat a room than an open fireplace), bifocal spectacles, and several other ingenious devices. [7]_____ he served 14 years (1751–1764) in the Pennsylvania assembly. [8]He founded a circulating library and helped get the first hospital in Philadelphia built. [9]He came up with the idea of a lottery to raise money for public purposes. [10]In his spare time he taught himself Latin, French, Spanish, and Italian.

Franklin wrote so much about the virtues of hard work and thrift that some historians have described him as stuffy and straitlaced. [12]Nothing could be further from the truth. [13]He recognized the social value of conventional behavior, but he was no slave to convention. [14]He wrote satirical essays on such subjects as the advantage of having affairs with older women and plain-looking women (who were, he claimed, more likely to appreciate the attention). [15]And he had the perfect temperament, being open-minded and imaginative as well as shrewd and judicious—an unbeatable combination.

—Carnes and Garraty, *The American Nation*, 11th ed., p. 90.

_____ 1. Which of the following statements expresses the central point of the passage?
   a. American colonists contributed significantly to the world's collection of scientific knowledge.
   b. Some historians consider Benjamin Franklin as a stuffy and straitlaced colonist.
   c. Benjamin Franklin was a man of many talents who made significant contributions to colonial life.
   d. Benjamin Franklin had a perfect temperament, being open-minded and imaginative as well as shrewd and judicious.

_____ 2. The transition word that best fits the blank in sentence 6 is _____.
   a. also
   b. frequently
   c. first
   d. additional

_____ 3. The transition word that best fits the blank in sentence 7 is _____.
   a. moreover
   b. frequently
   c. third
   d. in addition

99

_____ 4. The thought pattern used in the first paragraph is _____.
   a. time order
   b. space order
   c. listing
   d. classification

_____ 5. The transition words that signal the pattern of thought are _____.
   a. *but*, and *as*
   b. *one example* and *such*
   c. *also, in addition, and*
   d. *produced, capped,* and *invented*

Paragraph B

[1]Perhaps the most puzzling of all animal societies are those of the bees, ants, and termites. [2]Scientists have long struggled to explain the evolution of a social structure in which most individuals never breed, but instead labor intensively to feed and protect the offspring of a different individual. [3]Individual social insects are born into one of several castes within their society. [4]These castes are groups of similar individuals that perform a specific function.

[5]Honeybees are one _____ of social insects. They emerge from their larval stage into one of three major preordained roles. [6]One _____ is that of *queen*. [7]Only one queen is tolerated in a hive at any time. [8]Her functions are to produce eggs (up to 1,000 per day for a lifetime of 5 to 10 years) and regulate the lives of the workers.

[9]Male bees, called *drones*, serve merely as mates for the queen. [10]Soon after the queen hatches, drones swarm around her, and she mates with as many as 15 of them. [11]This supplies her with sperm that will last a lifetime, enough to fertilize more than 3 million eggs. [12]Drones then become superfluous and are eventually driven out of the hive or killed.

[13]The hive is run by the third _____ of bees, sterile female *workers*. [14]A worker's tasks are determined by her age and by conditions in the colony. [15]Workers can be "waitresses," carrying food to the queen and other workers, "maids," cleaning the hive, or foragers, gathering pollen and nectar, food for the hive.

—Adapted from Audesirk, Audesirk, and Byers, *Life on Earth*, 5th ed., p. 527–528.

_____ 6. Which statement expresses the central idea of the passage?
   a. Honeybees are one kind of social insects whose individuals are born into one of several castes within their society.
   b. Scientists are often puzzled by the nature of animal and insect societies and sometimes find it hard to explain their social structure.
   c. Male bees are unfairly treated in the social strata of the honeybees.
   d. Worker bees are always females, and they do all of the work of running and maintaining the hive for the rest of the bee population.

_____ 7. The appropriate transition word for the blank in sentence 5 is _____.
   a. characteristic
   b. type
   c. second
   d. trait

____ 8. The appropriate transition word for the blank in sentence 6 is _____.
   a. moreover
   b. role
   c. stages
   d. kind

____ 9. The appropriate transition word for the blank in sentence 13 is _____.
   a. stage
   b. trait
   c. class
   d. function

____ 10. The primary thought pattern used in this final paragraph is _____
   a. time order
   b. space order
   c. listing
   d. classification

Chapter 7: Transitions and Thought Patterns
LAB 7.4 REVIEW TEST 2

Name_____ Section _____ Date _____ Score (number correct) _____ x 10 = _____

Directions: Read the passages and answer the questions that follow.

Paragraph A

Meditation and Stress

[1]Meditation takes many forms. [2]In its simplest form, it amounts to little more than calm thinking. [3]You can try this form of meditation, also referred to as breathing relaxation. [4]First, relax quietly with your eyes closed and focus on your breathing. [5]Each time you inhale, fill your lower abdomen with air first and, then, allow your stomach to expand upward _____ your chest is full of air. [6]Exhale at half the rate that you inhaled, slowly and completely, each time thinking about the word calm. [7]Stretch out the word so that it becomes caaaaaaallllllmmmmmmmm. [8]If thoughts arise or your attention wanders, simply focus on your breathing.

[9]_____ popular form of meditation is known as transcendental meditation (TM). [10]This type of meditation is an aspect of yoga which was made popular by the Maharishi Mahesh Yogi. [11]Transcendental meditation involves sitting upright in a comfortable position in a quiet place with eyes closed. [12]Then a secret mantra is mentally repeated (a mantra is a word or sound) _____ a passive mental state is maintained. [13]Unlike breathing relaxation, transcendental meditation requires much practice. [14]All forms of meditation are believed to invoke a relaxation response. [15]Research indicates that meditation is an effective way to manage stress.

—Adapted from Pruitt and Stein, *Health Styles*, 2nd ed., p. 90

_____ 1. What thought pattern does the first sentence suggest?
   a. time order
   b. classification
   c. space order

_____ 2. The relationship between sentence 4 and sentence 5 is one of _____.
   a. time order
   b. listing
   c. classification
   d. space order

_____ 3. The transition that best fits the blank in sentence 5 is _____.
   a. below
   b. next
   c. until
   d. following

_____ 4. The transition that best fits the blank in sentence 9 is _____.
   a. below
   b. next
   c. another
   d. while

_____ 5. The transition that best fits the blank in sentence 12 is _____.
   a. below
   b. while
   c. another
   d. during

_____ 6. The transition words that signal the main pattern of thought in this passage are _____.
   a. *this form, another popular form, type*
   b. *first, then*
   c. *each time*
   d. *if, unlike*

Paragraph B

[1]People do more than just behave. [2]There are feelings that accompany every human action, and emotions play a part in the way we feel about things in all of our daily activities. [3]Emotion can be defined as the "feeling" aspect of consciousness, characterized by three elements.

[4]The _____ element of emotion is physical arousal. [5]Physically, when a person experiences an emotion, an arousal is created by the sympathetic nervous system. [6]The heart rate increases, breathing becomes more rapid, the pupils dilate, and the mouth may become dry. [7]For example, when we become angry, there is an increase in skin temperature and a greater increase in blood pressure.

[8]Expression is the second element of emotion. [9]There are facial expressions body movements, and actions that indicate to others how a person feels. [10]Frowns, smiles and sad expressions combine with hand gestures, the turning of one's body, and spoken words to produce an understanding of emotion. [11]People fight, run, kiss, and yell, along with countless other actions stemming from the emotions they feel.

[12]Finally, the _____ element of emotion is interpreting the subjective feeling by giving it a label: anger, fear, disgust, happiness, sadness, shame, interest, and so on. [13]Another way of labeling this element is to call it the "cognitive element," because the labeling process is a matter of retrieving memories of previous similar experiences, perceiving the context of the emotion, and coming up with a solution—a label.

—Adapted from Ciccarelli and White, *Psychology*, 2nd ed., pp. 378-381.

_____ 7. Which statement expresses the central idea of the passage?
   a. People do more than just behave.
   b. There are feelings that accompany every human action, and emotions play a part in the way we feel about things in all of our daily activities.
   c. Physically, when a person experiences an emotion, an arousal is created by the sympathetic nervous system.
   d. Emotion can be defined as the "feeling" aspect of consciousness, characterized by three elements.

_____ 8. The appropriate transition word for the blank in sentence 4 is _____.
   a. first
   b. next
   c. second
   d. trait

103

____ 9. The appropriate transition word for the blank in sentence 12 is _____.
   a. end
   b. third
   c. best
   d. later

____ 10. The primary thought pattern used in this paragraph is _____
   a. time order
   b. space order
   c. listing
   d. classification

Name _____ Section _____ Date _____ Score (number correct) _____ x 10 = _____

Directions: Read the passage and answer the questions that follow.

A. [1]The basis of all stratification (ranking) systems in society is the judging of people according to their possession of things that are scarce and, therefore, highly prized. [2]These scarce resources almost always _____ class, status, and power. [3]It is according to these dimensions that people are assigned a rank in society and relegated to a stratum with others who are ranked similarly.

[4]Social class is _____ dimension of ranking systems. [5]Although discussions of social class figure prominently in the media and the term is commonly used in conversation, most people would have difficulty defining the term with accuracy. [6]Most Americans volunteer the information that they belong to the middle class, _____ they appear only slightly aware of the vast differences in lifestyles of different groups of people.

[7]Status, the second basis for the classification system, is the degree of social esteem that an individual or group enjoys in society. [8]Status may mean prestige rather than simply a position within the social system. [9]The most important element of status is that it is a ranked position—high, middle, low—determined by how the role attached to the status is valued.

[10]The final important dimension of stratification—some consider it the most important dimension—is power. [11]Power is defined as the ability to carry out one's wishes in spite of resistance. [12]It is the ability to get other people to do what one wants them to do, with or without their consent. [13]Power is exercised in all social systems, from the simplest to the most complex.

—Adapted from Perry and Perry, *Contemporary Society: An Introduction to Social Science*, 12th ed., pp. 162–164.

_____ 1. The central idea of this passage is expressed in _____.
   a. the first paragraph
   b. the second paragraph
   c. the third paragraph
   d. the fourth paragraph

_____ 2. Which transitions signal the thought pattern of this paragraph?
   a. *similarly* and *differences*
   b. *simplest* and *complex*
   c. *classification* and *most important*
   d. *one*, *second*, and *final*

_____ 3. How many major points support the main idea on this passage?
   a. one
   b. two
   c. three
   d. four

_____ 4. In general, the major details of this passage _____.
   a. list problems associated with ranking systems
   b. list the dimensions used to rank individuals in a society
   c. classify societies according to their ranking systems
   d. compare societies based upon their ranking systems

_____ 5. The thought pattern used in the passage is _____.
   a. space order
   b. time order
   c. listing order
   d. classification

_____ 6. The appropriate transition word for the blank in sentence 2 is _____.
   a. characteristic
   b. type
   c. second
   d. include

_____ 7. The appropriate transition word for the blank in sentence 4 is _____.
   a. moreover
   b. one
   c. stages
   d. kind

_____ 8. The appropriate transition word for the blank in sentence 6 is _____.
   a. instead
   b. and
   c. class
   d. after

_____ 9. The transition word *second* in sentence 7 signals _____.
   a. addition
   b. time
   c. space
   d. classification

_____ 10. The transition word *final* signals _____.
   a. addition
   b. time
   c. space
   d. classification

Chapter 7: Transitions and Thought Patterns
LAB 7.6 MASTERY TEST 2

Name_____Section _____ Date _____ Score (number correct) _____ x 10 = _____

Directions: Read the paragraphs and answer the questions that follow.

Paragraph A

[1]Although violence has long been a concern in American society, not until 1985 did the U.S. Public Health Service formally identify violence as a leading public-health problem that contributes significantly to death and disability rates. [2]_____ 1973, statistics from the Federal Bureau of Investigation (FBI) had shown that, overall, crime and certain types of violent crime have decreased each year. [3]However, between January and June 2006, violent crime was up by 3.7 percent when compared to the same period in 2005 in all major regions of the country. [4]Overall rates of violent crime actually increased by 2.5 percent overall, and murder specifically increased by nearly 5 percent in 2005 over the previous year.

—Adapted from Donatelle, *Health: the Basics*, 8th ed., p. 91.

_____ 1. The main idea of this paragraph is expressed in _____.
    a. sentence 1
    b. sentence 2
    c. sentence 3
    d. sentence 4

_____ 2. The appropriate transition word for the blank in sentence 2 is _____.
    a. once
    b. later
    c. since
    d. during

_____ 3. In general, the major details of this paragraph _____.
    a. list problems associated with the increase in violence
    b. list the factors that are thought to cause the rise in violence
    c. compares the violence in the United States to other countries
    d. show the increase in violence since it was noted as a public-health problem in 1973

_____ 4. Which of the following transitions signal the thought pattern of this paragraph?
    a. *although* and *however*
    b. *decreased* and *increased*
    c. *until*, *between*, *period*, and *previous*
    d. *types* and *compared*

_____ 5. The thought pattern used in the passage is _____.
    a. space order
    b. time order
    c. listing order
    d. classification

Paragraph B

[1]The North Atlantic and the northeastern and southern Pacific are known for stormy weather, and these storms bring plenty of moisture to the adjacent land areas. [2]Midlatitude cyclones are frequent, especially in winter. [3]The low temperatures mean that air contains less moisture than at lower latitudes, so drizzle is common. [4]Annual rainfall is about 70 to 120 centimeters (28 to 47 inches). [5]Where mountains are _____ the coast, as in western North America, Chile, and Norway, the height of the land contributes to high rainfall, 2 to 3 meters (6 to 9 feet) per year. [6]The current highest average annual rainfall in the mainland United States is in a marine climate—the west coast of the Olympic Peninsula in Washington, where annual rainfall totals 3 to 4 meters (10 to 13 feet).

—Adapted from Bergman and Renwick, *Introduction to Geography: People, Places, and Environment,*
4th ed., p. 81.

_____ 6. The main idea is expressed in _____.
   a. sentence 1
   b. sentence 2
   c. sentence 4
   d. sentence 6

_____ 7. In general the main points of this paragraph _____.
   a. describe the difficulties of living in a rainy climate
   b. classify the levels of rainfall around the world
   c. analyze the characteristics of mountainous areas in the North Atlantic
   d. describe the climate in the North Atlantic and the northeastern and southern Pacific

_____ 8. The appropriate transition word for the blank in sentence 5 is _____.
   a. under
   b. beneath
   c. near
   d. before

_____ 9. The thought pattern used in the paragraph is
   a. classification
   b. listing
   c. time order
   d. space order

_____ 10. The transition words that signal this pattern are _____.
   a. *effects contribute*
   b. *adjacent, lower, where*
   c. *frequent* and *annual*
   d. *and, contains,* and *totals*

Chapter 8: More Thought Patterns
LAB 8.1 PRACTICE EXERCISE 1

Name_____ Section _____ Date _____ Score (number correct) _____ x 10 = _____

Objective: To use transitions and thought patterns.

Directions: Read each paragraph and answer the questions that follow.

[1]Cultures vary widely in their responses to physical and verbal abuse. [2]In some Asian and Hispanic cultures, for example, the fear of losing face or embarrassing the family is so great that people prefer not to report or reveal abuses. [3]When looking over statistics, it may at first appear that little violence occurs in the families of certain cultures. [4]Yet we know from research that wife beating is quite common in India, Taiwan, and Iran, for example. [5]In much of the United States, and in many other cultures as well, such abuse would not be tolerated no matter who was embarrassed or insulted.

—DeVito, *The Interpersonal Communication Book*, 10th ed., p. 313.

_____ 1. Which sentence states the main idea of the paragraph?
   a. sentence 1
   b. sentence 2
   c. sentence 3
   d. sentence 5

_____ 2. What contrast transition word is used to show differing views of abuse in various countries?
   a. for example
   b. first
   c. yet
   d. as well

[1]Each culture seems to teach its members different views of conflict strategies. [2]In one study, African American females were found to use more direct controlling strategies (for example, assuming control over the conflict and arguing persistently for their point of view) than did white females. [3]White females, _____, used more solution-oriented conflict styles than did African American females. [4]Another example of this cultural influence on conflict is seen in the tendency of collectivist cultures to avoid conflict more than members of individualist cultures.

—DeVito, *The Interpersonal Communication Book*, 10th ed. p. 313.

_____ 3. Which sentence states the main idea of the paragraph?
   a. sentence 1
   b. sentence 2
   c. sentence 3
   d. sentence 5

_____ 4. The most appropriate transition for the blank in sentence 3 is _____.
   a. further
   b. similarly
   c. differ
   d. on the other hand

_____ 5. Which phrase in sentence 4 signals a comparison-contrast relationship?
    a. another example
    b. of this cultural influence
    c. on conflict
    d. more than

_____ 6. The primary pattern of organization for the paragraph is _____.
    a. cause and effect
    b. example
    c. comparison and contrast
    d. definition

Armed with an indictment (or an *information* filed on the basis of the preliminary hearing outcome in states not requiring grand jury proceedings), the prosecutor files the case against the accused in felony court (variably called a *district, superior*, or *common pleas court*), which sets a date for arraignment. The arraignment proceeding is the first time defendants (the accused's status has changed from suspect to defendant on the basis of the indictment or information) have had the opportunity to respond to the charges against them. After the charges are read to the defendant, he or she must then enter a formal response to them, known as a *plea*.

—Ellis and Walsh, *Criminology*, 2000, pp. 564, 516

_____ 7. Which concept map best indicates the cause-and-effect pattern used in this paragraph?

a.

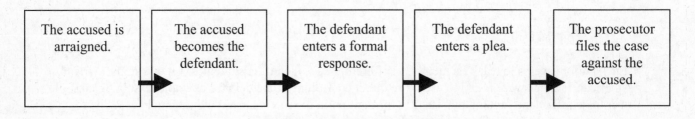

b.

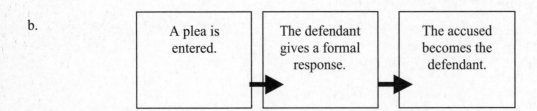

c.

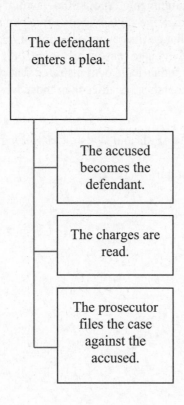

d.

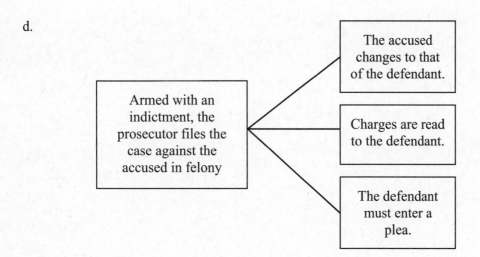

[1]The plea alternatives are guilty, not guilty, or no contest (*nolo contendere*). [2]A guilty plea is usually the result of a plea bargain agreement concluded before the arraignment. [3]About 90 percent of all felony cases in the United States are settled by plea bargains in which the state extends some benefit to the defendant (e.g., reduced charges, a lighter sentence) in exchange for his or her cooperation. [4]By pleading guilty, defendants give up their rights to be proven guilty "beyond a reasonable doubt," their right against self-incrimination, and their right to appeal. [5]A number of studies have demonstrated that defendants who insist on their constitutional right to a trial are subjected to harsher penalties than those who plead guilty by a system that relies on plea bargains to keep functioning.

—Ellis and Walsh, *Criminology*, 2000, p. 564.

_____ 8. Which sentence states the main idea of the paragraph?
      a. sentence 1
      b. sentence 2
      c. sentence 3
      d. sentence 5

_____ 9. The details of this paragraph indicate the _____.
      a. causes of a guilty plea
      b. definition of *nolo contendere*
      c. consequences of a not guilty plea
      d. consequences of guilty and not guilty plea

_____ 10. Which word from the paragraph signals an effect?
      a. alternatives
      b. result
      c. settled
      d. reduced

Chapter 8: More Thought Patterns
LAB 8.2 PRACTICE EXERCISE 2

Name_____ Section _____ Date _____ Score (number correct) _____ x 10 = _____

Objective: To use transitions correctly and to identify patterns of thought.

Directions: Read the following paragraphs from a college nutrition textbook. Fill in the blanks in each paragraph with the appropriate transition words or phrases. Then, answer the questions following the paragraph.

[1]Travelers' diarrhea is experienced by people traveling to countries outside of their own and is usually _____ by viral or bacterial infections. [2]Diarrhea represents the body's way of ridding itself of the invasive agent. [3]The irritation of the intestines by microbes leads to increased secretion of fluid, _____ watery stools and higher than normal frequency of bowel movements.

—Adapted from Thompson and Manore, *Nutrition: An Applied Approach*, 2nd ed., p. 108.

_____ 1. The most appropriate transition for the blank in sentence 1 is _____.
   a. different
   b. on the other hand
   c. caused
   d. compared

_____ 2. The most appropriate transition for the blank in sentence 3 is _____.
   a. different from
   b. compared to
   c. as
   d. resulting in

_____ 3. The primary thought pattern expressed in this paragraph is _____.
   a. cause and effect
   b. definition
   c. comparison and contrast
   d. generalization and example

[1]Society is defined as the largest group of people inhabiting a specific territory and sharing a common way of life (culture). [2]The people in a society share this common way of life as a result of interacting on a regular, continuous basis and because they have acquired patterns of behavior on which all more or less agree. [3]Society differs from many other large groups because within this group people can live a total, common life, whereas in smaller groups a person lives only one facet of her or his life. [4]In short, society is not an organization limited to a specific purpose, as is, for example, the American Medical Association. [5]Rather, it is the most self-sufficient group, and its independence is based on the techniques developed to fulfill the needs of its members.

—Adapted from Perry and Perry, *Contemporary Society: An Introduction to Social Science*, 12th ed., p. 87.

_____ 4. The word *defined* in sentence 1 signals _____.
   a. comparison
   b. definition
   c. contrast
   d. cause and effect

113

____ 5. The word *result* in sentence 2 signals _____.
   a. comparison
   b. definition
   c. contrast
   d. cause and effect

____ 6. The word *differs* in sentence 3 signals _____.
   a. comparison
   b. definition
   c. contrast
   d. cause and effect

____ 7. The relationship between sentence 4 and sentence 5 is _____.
   a. cause and effect
   b. definition and example
   c. contrast
   d. generalization and example

____ 8. The thought patterns used in the paragraph are definition and _____.
   a. cause and effect
   b. generalization and example
   c. comparison
   d. contrast

[1]While marriage may never have been out of fashion, it has frequently taken forms that today's Americans would not recognize. [2]For instance, marriage could be a relationship between one husband and more than one wife, polygamy, as practiced in early Judaism, Islam, nineteenth-century Mormonism, pre-modern China, and parts of Africa. [3]Marriage could also involve one wife with several husbands, polyandry, as occurred in Tibet. [4]Other more rare forms of marriage include sequential marriages of a widow to brothers, as practiced in ancient Judaism, and the marriage of female husbands to female wives, as practiced in some African societies.

—Adapted from Edgar, Hackett, Jewsbury, Molony, and Gordon,
Civilizations Past & Present, Vol. II, from 1300, 12th ed., p. 1096.

____ 9. The relationship between sentence 1 and sentence 2 is _____.
   a. cause and effect
   b. example
   c. comparison
   d. contrast

____ 10. The primary thought pattern in the paragraph is _____.
   a. cause and effect
   b. generalization and example
   c. comparison and contrast
   d. definition

114

Name_____ Section _____ Date _____ Score (number correct) _____ x 10 = _____

Objective: To use transitions correctly and to identify patterns of thought.

Directions: Read the paragraphs and answer the questions that follow.

[1]Cultures _____ in how they define what constitutes conflict. [2]_____, in some cultures it's quite common for women to be referred to negatively and as less than equal. [3]To most people in the United States, this would constitute a clear basis for conflict. [4]To some Japanese women, _____, this isn't uncommon and isn't perceived as abusive (*New York Times*, 11 February 1996, pp. 1, 12). [5]_____, Americans and Japanese differ in their view of the aim or purpose of conflict. [6]The Japanese see conflicts and their resolution in terms of compromise; Americans, _____, see conflict in terms of winning.

—Adapted from DeVito, *The Interpersonal Communication Book,* 10th ed., p. 313.

____ 1. The most appropriate transition for the blank in sentence 1 is _____.
   a. however
   b. for example
   c. differ
   d. on the other hand

____ 2. The most appropriate transition for the blank in sentence 2 is _____.
   a. however
   b. for example
   c. differ
   d. on the other hand

____ 3. The most appropriate transition for the blank in sentence 4 is _____.
   a. however
   b. for example
   c. differ
   d. on the other hand

____ 4. The most appropriate transition for the blank in sentence 5 is _____.
   a. however
   b. for example
   c. differ
   d. further

____ 5. The most appropriate transition for the blank in sentence 6 is _____.
   a. however
   b. for example
   c. differ
   d. on the other hand

_____ 6. The transition used to fill the blank in sentence 1 signals _____.
   a. comparison and contrast
   b. cause and effect
   c. example
   d. definition

_____ 7. The transition used to fill the blank in sentence 2 signals _____.
   a. comparison and contrast
   b. cause and effect
   c. generalization and example
   d. definition

_____ 8. The transition used to fill the blank in sentence 4 signals _____.
   a. comparison and contrast
   b. cause and effect
   c. addition
   d. definition

_____ 9. The transition used to fill the blank in sentence 5 signals _____.
   a. comparison and contrast
   b. cause and effect
   c. generalization and example
   d. addition

___ 10. The transition used to fill the blank in sentence 6 signals _____.
   a. comparison and contrast
   b. cause and effect
   c. generalization and example
   d. addition

Chapter 8: More Thought Patterns
LAB 8.4 REVIEW TEST 2

Name_____Section_____Date_____Score (number correct)_____ x 10 = _____

Directions: Read the paragraphs and answer the questions that follow.

[1]Male and female college students have _____ expectations regarding their areas of competence. [2]_____, one survey asked first-year college students whether they were above or below average on a variety of traits and abilities. [3]Men were more likely than women to think of themselves as above average in overall academic and mathematical ability, competitiveness, and emotional health.

[4]Both male and female college professors treat men and women differently in their classes, as well, even though the different treatment is largely unintentional and often the professors are unaware of their actions. [5]For instance, professors call on men in class more frequently than on women, and they make more eye contact with men _____ with women. [6]_____, male students are more likely than women to receive extra help from their professors. [7]Finally, the male students often receive more positive reinforcement for their comments than female students do.

—Adapted from Ciccarelli and White, *Psychology*, 2nd ed., p. 373.

_____ 1. This selection describes _____.
   a. differences between men and women
   b. similarities between men and women on a college campus
   c. differences between men and women on a college campus
   d. relations between men and women on a college campus

_____ 2. The most appropriate transition for the blank in sentence 1 is _____.
   a. however
   b. different
   c. similar
   d. on the other hand

_____ 3. The transition used to fill the blank in sentence 1 signals a(n) _____ relationship.
   a. comparison and contrast
   b. cause and effect
   c. example
   d. definition

_____ 4. The most appropriate transition for the blank in sentence 2 is _____.
   a. however
   b. meanwhile
   c. for example
   d. after

_____ 5. The transition used to fill the bank in sentence 2 signals a(n) _____.
   a. comparison and contrast
   b. cause and effect relationship
   c. additional difference
   d. example of the previous thought

117

____ 6. The most appropriate transition for the blank in sentence 5 is _____.
   a. however
   b. for example
   c. differ
   d. than

____ 7. The transition used to fill the bank in sentence 5 signals a(n) _____ relationship.
   a. comparison and contrast
   b. cause and effect
   c. example
   d. definition

____ 8. The most appropriate transition for the blank in sentence 6 is _____.
   a. for example
   b. furthermore
   c. while
   d. on the other hand

____ 9. The transition used to fill the bank in sentence 6 signals a(n) _____ relationship.
   a. comparison and contrast
   b. cause and effect relationship
   c. additional difference
   d. definition

___ 10. The primary pattern of organization for the paragraph is _____.
   a. cause and effect
   b. example
   c. comparison and contrast
   d. definition

Name_____ Section _____ Date _____ Score (number correct) _____ x 10 = _____

A. Directions: Read each of the following passages and identify the pattern of thought.

Children around the world are suffering needlessly from lack of food. To illustrate this point, consider children living in impoverished conditions who are fed diluted cereal drinks that are inadequate in energy, protein, and most nutrients. Many of these children are suffering from a disease called marasmus and are slowly starving to death.

—Adapted from Thompson and Manore, *Nutrition: An Applied Approach,*
2nd ed., p. 242.

_____ 1.   The primary pattern of thought is _____.
a.   generalization and example
b.   comparison
c.   cause and effect
d.   definition and example

_____ 2.   Which word from the paragraph signals the primary pattern of thought?
a.   *around*
b.   *to illustrate*
c.   *inadequate*
d.   *many*

African American and white men are similar in the way they handle conflicts; both often avoid or withdraw from relationship conflicts, preferring to keep quiet about their differences or make them seem insignificant.

—Adapted from DeVito, *The Interpersonal Communication Book,* 10th ed., p. 313.

_____ 3.   The primary pattern of thought is _____.
a.   cause and effect
b.   comparison
c.   generalization and example
d.   contrast

_____ 4.   Which word from the paragraph signals the primary pattern of thought?
a.   *similar*
b.   *often*
c.   *differences*
d.   *insignificant*

B. Directions: Read the following paragraph and answer the questions that follow.

[1]Besides basic emotions, humans are capable of a second, higher order set of feelings, including shame, embarrassment, guilt, envy, and pride. [2]These are called *self-conscious emotions* because each involves

119

injury to or enhancement of our sense of self. [3]For example, when we are ashamed or embarrassed, we feel negatively about our behavior, and we want to retreat so others will no longer notice our failings. [4]In contrast, pride reflects delight in the self's achievements, and we are inclined to tell others what we have accomplished.

—Berk, *Development Through the Lifespan*, 3rd ed., p. 179.

_____ 5. The phrase *are called* in sentence 2 signals _____.
    a. a definition
    b. a comparison
    c. a contrast
    d. a cause and effect

_____ 6. The phrase *because* in sentence 2 signals _____.
    a. a definition
    b. a comparison
    c. a contrast
    d. a cause and effect

_____ 7. The relationship between sentence 3 and sentence 4 is one of _____.
    a. cause and effect
    b. comparison
    c. generalization and example
    d. contrast

_____ 8. The primary pattern of organization for the paragraph is _____.
    a. cause and effect
    b. comparison
    c. definition and example
    d. contrast

C. Directions: Read the following paragraph and answer the questions that follow.

[1]Caffeine is the most popular and widely consumed drug in the United States.[2]When the effects of a cup of coffee wear off, users may feel let down—mentally or physically depressed, exhausted, and weak. [3]To counteract this let-down, people commonly choose to drink another cup of coffee. [4]Habitually engaging in this practice leads to tolerance and psychological dependence. [5]Until the mid 1970s, chronic caffeine use and its attendant behaviors were called "coffee nerves." [6]This syndrome is now recognized as caffeine intoxication.

—Adapted from Donatelle, *Health: the Basics*, 8th ed., p. 242–243.

_____ 9. The primary thought pattern is _____.
    a. definition
    b. comparison and contrast
    c. example and example
    d. cause and effect

_____ 10. The word from the paragraph that signals the primary thought pattern is _____.
    a. *when*
    b. *leads to*
    c. *until*
    d. *now*

Name _____ Section _____ Date _____ Score (number correct) _____ x 10 = _____

Objective: To use transitions correctly and to identify patterns of thought.

A. Directions: Read each of the following passages and answer the questions that follow.

About three generations ago William Ogburn (1922/1938), a functional analyst, coined the term **cultural lag**. By this, Ogburn meant that not all parts of a culture change at the same pace. When some part of a culture changes, other parts lag behind.

Ogburn points out that *a group's material culture usually changes first, with the nonmaterial culture lagging behind*, playing a game of catch up. For example, when we get sick, we could type our symptoms into a computer and get an immediate printout of our diagnosis and the best course of treatment. In fact, in some tests, computers outperform physicians. Yet our customs have not caught up with our technology, and we continue to visit the doctor's office.

—Henslin, *Essentials of Sociology*, 5th ed., p. 50.

____ 1. The primary thought pattern is _____.
  a. cause and effect
  b. definition and example
  c. comparison and contrast
  d. generalization and example

____ 2. The word or phrase from the passage that signals the thought pattern is _____.
  a. *coined* and *for example*
  b. *ago* and *behind*
  c. *same* and *best*
  d. *yet*

Peer sociability in collectivist societies takes different forms than in individualistic cultures. For example, children in India generally play in large groups that require high levels of cooperation. Much of their behavior during sociodramatic play and early games is imitative, occurs in unison, and involves close physical contact. In a game called Bhatto Bhatto, children act out a script about a trip to the market, touching each other's elbows and hands as they pretend to cut and share a tasty vegetable

—Berk, *Development Through the Lifespan*, 3rd ed., p. 250.

____ 3. The primary thought pattern is _____.
  a. cause and effect
  b. definition and example
  c. comparison and contrast
  d. generalization and example

_____ 4. The word or phrase from the passage that signals the thought pattern is _____.
   a. *than*
   b. *for example* and *generally*
   c. *different*
   d. *for example*

Researchers often find four patterns of changes in self-esteem in teenagers. The largest group of teens display consistently high self-esteem throughout adolescence. The second group, however, exhibit low self-esteem early in adolescence, but it rises steadily as they get older. The self-esteem ratings of the third group are low in both early and late adolescent. Teens in the fourth group enjoy moderate to high self-esteem at the beginning of the period but exhibit steady declines as adolescence progresses. As you might suspect, differences in self-esteem are related to some important developmental outcomes.

—Adapted from Bee and Boyd, *The Developing Child*, 11th.ed., p. 289.

_____ 5. The primary thought pattern is _____.
   a. cause and effect
   b. definition and example
   c. comparison and contrast
   d. generalization and example

_____ 6. The word or phrase from the passage that signals the thought pattern is _____.
   a. *often*
   b. *patterns*
   c. *however* and *but*
   d. *second group*

B. Directions: Read the following paragraphs and answer the questions that follow.

Case Study: Unfair Advantage

[1]On a sunny July morning in 1998, the members of the Festina bicycle racing team, the top-rated team in the world, sat in a French café. [2]Nearby, dozens of other professional bicyclists made their final preparations for the impending start of the day's segment of the grueling Tour de France race. [3]The Festina riders, however, would not be joining the race. [4]Hours earlier, the entire team had been expelled from the Tour de France for the offense of blood doping.

[5]The dramatic expulsion of top athletes from the world's premier bicycle race focused attention on the arcane practice of blood doping. [6]By using blood-doping techniques, some athletes try to gain a competitive edge. [7]But what is blood doping, and how does it affect athletic performance?

[8]Blood doping increases a person's physical endurance by increasing the capacity of the blood to carry oxygen. [9]One crude method for accomplishing this goal is to simply inject extra red blood cells into the bloodstream. [10]Red blood cells transport oxygen to the body's tissues, so simply adding more of them is a straightforward way of increasing the amount of oxygen that reaches the tissues. [11]In recent years, however, blood-doping athletes have increasingly turned to injections of erythropoietin (EPO) as a more effective approach to increasing blood oxygen.

[12]EPO is a protein molecule that is present in a normal human body, where it functions as a chemical messenger that stimulates bone marrow to produce more red blood cells. [13]Under normal circumstances, the body produces just enough EPO to ensure that red blood cells are replaced as they age and die. [14]An injection of extra EPO, however, can stimulate the production of a huge number of extra red blood cells. [15]The extra cells greatly increase the oxygen-carrying capacity of the blood. [16]Unfortunately, the excess blood cells also thicken the blood and make it harder to move through blood vessels, so those who inject EPO suffer increased risk of heart failure.

[17]Why would professional athletes take such a risk to get more oxygen molecules into their bloodstream? [18]How does extra oxygen increase endurance? [19]The answers to those questions lie in the role of oxygen in supplying energy to muscle cells.

—Adapted from Audersirk, Audersirk, and Byers, *Life on Earth*, 3rd ed., p. 955.

_____ 7. Which sentence from paragraph 1 contains a contrast transition?
   a. sentence 1
   b. sentence 2
   c. sentence 3
   d. sentence 4

_____ 8. The relationship of sentence 11 to sentence 10 is one of _____.
   a. comparison
   b. cause and effect
   c. example
   d. contrast

_____ 9. The phrase *more effective* in sentence 11 signals a _____.
   a. definition
   b. comparison
   c. contrast
   d. causes and effect

_____ 10. The primary pattern of thought in this passage is _____.
   a. cause and effect
   b. generalization and example
   c. definition and example

123

Chapter 9: Fact and Opinion
LAB 9.1 PRACTICE EXERCISE 1

Name_____Section _____ Date _____ Score (number correct) _____ x 10 = _____

Objective: To identify an author's use of facts and opinions in reading passages.

A. Directions: Read the following selection and determine whether each sentence is a fact, an opinion, or a combination of both.

Never Too Clean

Heather and Jean were working side by side in the kitchen preparing dinner. Heather was meticulous about hygiene. She filled the sink with piping hot, soapy water and scrubbed the kitchen knives, all the counter-tops, and cutting boards with surprising energy.

"That water is too hot," Jean exclaimed, "You are going to ruin your beautiful hands."

"Well," Heather replied, "I read in the paper that washing hands in hot soapy water for at least 20 seconds rinses off surface bacteria and makes it difficult for bacteria to cling to skin. So I think, if it's smart to wash your hands, it's probably smart to wash the work space and utensils, too."

"You are a little paranoid about a few germs, aren't you?" Jean asked.

"With something this important, it doesn't hurt to be cautious," Heather answered.

_____1. Heather and Jean were working side by side in the kitchen preparing dinner.
    a. fact
    b. opinion
    c. combination of fact and opinion

_____2. Heather was meticulous about hygiene.
    a. fact
    b. opinion
    c. combination of fact and opinion

_____3. She filled the sink with piping hot, soapy water and scrubbed the kitchen knives, all the counter-tops, and cutting boards with surprising energy.
    a. fact
    b. opinion
    c. combination of fact and opinion

_____4. "That water is too hot," Jean exclaimed, "You are going to ruin your beautiful hands."
    a. fact
    b. opinion
    c. combination of fact and opinion

_____5. "Well," Heather replied, "I read in the paper that washing hands in hot soapy water for at least 20 seconds rinses off surface bacteria and makes it difficult for bacteria to cling to skin.
   a. fact
   b. opinion
   c. combination of fact and opinion

_____6. So I think, if it's smart to wash your hands, it's probably smart to wash the work space and utensils, too?"
   a. fact
   b. opinion
   c. combination of fact and opinion

_____7. "You are a little paranoid about a few germs, aren't you?" Jean asked.
   a. fact
   b. opinion
   c. combination of fact and opinion

B. Directions: Read the list of sources from which information can be obtained. Decide if each source is an informed opinion, an expert opinion, or a factual source.

_____8. A Harvard business major who is a financial analyst for the *Wall Street Journal*.
   a. informed opinion
   b. expert opinion
   c. factual source

_____9. Matthew Berry, former Hollywood screenwriter, who is now an ESPM Fantasy expert who provides daily fantasy football players with previews, game overviews, and injury reports and strategies.
   a. informed opinion
   b. expert opinion
   c. factual source

_____10. The McGraw-Hill *Concise Encyclopedia of Science and Technology*, a science reference that covers more than 90 disciplines of science and technology.
   a. informed opinion
   b. expert opinion
   c. factual source

Chapter 9: Fact and Opinion
LAB 9.2 PRACTICE EXERCISE 2

Name_____ Section _____ Date _____ Score (number correct) _____ x 10 = _____

Objective: To identify an author's use of facts and opinions in reading passages.

A. Directions: Read the statements and decide if they are facts, opinions, or a combination of fact and opinion.

_____ 1. This past winter, snowdrifts in New England reached heights of 42 feet.
    a. fact
    b. opinion
    c. combination of fact and opinion

_____ 2. On February 24, 1821, Mexico declared its independence from Spain.
    a. fact
    b. opinion
    c. combination of fact and opinion

_____ 3. Cal Ripken, Jr. never played any position other than shortstop and third base while in the majors; however, he was originally scouted as a pitcher.
    a. fact
    b. opinion
    c. combination of fact and opinion

_____ 4. It is often said that you have to be a "dog" to be a catcher because the position brings with it a lot of injuries and wear and tear on the knees.
    a. fact
    b. opinion
    c. combination of fact and opinion

_____ 5. I doubt if Cal Ripken, Jr. would have ever set the record for consecutive games played (the Iron Man record) had he been a catcher for many games; not to mention the fact that the Orioles' management should have their heads examined if they had put him in that position and risked ending that record-breaking streak of 2,100+ straight games without missing one!
    a. fact
    b. opinion
    c. combination of fact and opinion

_____ 6. People who are against smoking sound like Adolph Hitler, who had planned to ban smoking in Germany in order to promote the health of the Aryan race.
    a. fact
    b. opinion
    c. combination of fact and opinion

_____ 7. Citizens should not view taxation as a penalty, but as an opportunity to pool their money to enhance their quality of life.
    a. fact
    b. opinion
    c. combination of fact and opinion

B. Directions: Read the following paragraph and answer the questions that follow.

[1]The United States devoted a large part of its attention to the pursuit of the Cold War for most of the half century after the end of World War II. [2]It had emerged from World War II with its landscape unscathed and its economy the most powerful in the world. [3]Harry Truman served as president part of this time from 1945 to 1953.

—Adapted from Edgar, Hackett, Jewsbury, Molony, and Gordon, *Civilizations Past & Present, Vol. II, From 1300*, 12th ed., p. 989.

_____ 8. Sentence 1 is an example of _____.
    a. fact
    b. opinion
    c. combination of fact and opinion

_____ 9. Sentence 2 is an example of _____.
    a. fact
    b. opinion
    c. combination of fact and opinion

_____ 10. Sentence 3 is an example of _____.
    a. fact
    b. opinion
    c. combination of fact and opinion

Chapter 9: Fact and Opinion
LAB 9.3 REVIEW TEST 1

Name_____ Section _____ Date _____ Score (number correct) _____ x 10 = _____

A. Directions: Read the statements and decide if they are facts, opinions, or a combination of fact and opinion.

_____ 1. Recently, *Rover*, the roaming robot on Mars, discovered bedrock and minerals that could have been the site of water on the planet.
   a. fact
   b. opinion
   c. combination of fact and opinion

_____ 2. Politics is about illusions and revenge.
   a. fact
   b. opinion
   c. combination of fact and opinion

_____ 3. On February 24, 1868, the House of Representatives impeached President Andrew Johnson after he tried to dismiss Edwin M. Stanton, the Secretary of War, but the Senate later acquitted the president.
   a. fact
   b. opinion
   c. combination of fact and opinion

_____ 4. Henry A. Kissinger, a former U.S. Secretary of State, once said, "Nothing is more difficult for Americans to understand than the possibility of tragedy."
   a. fact
   b. opinion
   c. combination of fact and opinion

_____ 5. School policies should allow for common sense when it comes to the six-year-old who brought toy swords to school.
   a. fact
   b. opinion
   c. combination of fact and opinion

_____ 6. *Big Fish*, 2003, (PG-13) Violence, some images of nudity, and sexual references. Directed by Tim Burton, *Big Fish* is a story that is part fantasy and part family drama about a son's trying to understand his father. Although the complicated plot is at times difficult to follow, the magical touch of director Tim Burton makes the film worth seeing.
   a. fact
   b. opinion
   c. combination of fact and opinion

_____ 7. **Loews Ventana Canyon Resort.** Located at the base of the Catalina Mountains adjacent to Sabino Canyon in Coronado National Forest outside of Tucson, Arizona. The resort sits on 93 acres of desert with an 80-foot waterfall. The hotel overlooks two 18-hole Tom Fazio-designed PGA golf courses.
   a. fact
   b. opinion
   c. combination of fact and opinion

B. Directions: Read the following paragraph and answer the questions that follow.

[1]Announcing that the "Chinese people have now stood up," Mao Zedong proclaimed the founding of the People's Republic of China on October 1, 1949. [2]Decades of war and revolution were then to give way to nation-building. [3]But the trajectory of China's nation-building in the next half century was anything but smooth.

—Edgar, Hackett, Jewsbury, Molony, and Gordon, *Civilizations Past & Present, Vol. II, From 1300*, 12th ed., p.1048.

_____ 8. Sentence 1 is an example of _____.
   a. fact
   b. opinion
   c. combination of fact and opinion

_____ 9. Sentence 2 is an example of _____.
   a. fact
   b. opinion
   c. combination of fact and opinion

_____ 10. Sentence 3 is an example of _____.
   a. fact
   b. opinion
   c. combination of fact and opinion

Name_____ Section _____ Date _____ Score (number correct) _____ x 10 = _____

Directions: Read the following selection and determine whether each sentence is a fact, an opinion, or a combination of both.

Milestone Year in the History of Anabolic Steroids

[1]Two events in 1988 made that year a turning point in the history of anabolic steroids in sports. [2]The media had been exposing the widespread use of steroids since 1969. [3]But public interest was only briefly sparked, and media coverage would quickly dwindle. [4]Then, in September 1988, in a dramatic moment in the Seoul Olympic Games, the Canadian sprinter Ben Johnson won the gold medal in the men's 100-meter dash. [5]His time of 9.79 seconds broke world records. [6]Yet, he was denied his win. [7]He had tested positive for anabolic steroids. [8]Then about a month later, another dramatic fact became known. [9]The *Journal of the American Medical Association* reported the results of the first national survey on the use of anabolic steroids. [10]The survey found that around 7 percent of all high school seniors were using or had used anabolic steroids.

　　　　　　—Adapted from Levinthal, *Drugs, Behavior, and Modern Society*, 3rd ed., p. 171.

_____1.　Sentence 1 is a(n) _____.
　　a.　fact
　　b.　opinion
　　c.　combination of fact and opinion

_____2.　Sentence 2 is a(n) _____.
　　a.　fact
　　b.　opinion
　　c.　combination of fact and opinion

_____3.　Sentence 3 is a(n) _____.
　　a.　fact
　　b.　opinion
　　c.　combination of fact and opinion

_____4.　Sentence 4 is a(n) _____.
　　a.　fact
　　b.　opinion
　　c.　combination of fact and opinion

_____5.　Sentence 5 is a(n) _____.
　　a.　fact
　　b.　opinion
　　c.　combination of fact and opinion

_____ 6. Sentence 6 is a(n) _____.
   a. fact
   b. opinion
   c. combination of fact and opinion

_____ 7. Sentence 7 is a(n) _____.
   a. fact
   b. opinion
   c. combination of fact and opinion

_____ 8. Sentence 8 is a(n) _____.
   a. fact
   b. opinion
   c. combination of fact and opinion

_____ 9. Sentence 9 is a(n) _____.
   a. fact
   b. opinion
   c. combination of fact and opinion

_____ 10. Sentence 10 is a(n) _____.
   a. fact
   b. opinion
   c. combination of fact and opinion

Name_____ Section _____ Date _____ Score (number correct) _____ x 10 = _____

A. Directions: Read the statements and decide if they are facts, opinions, or a combination of fact and opinion.

_____ 1. The philosopher Thomas Hobbes (1588-1679) also presumed that all humans are fundamentally mean-spirited and brutish animals.
   a. fact
   b. opinion
   c. combination of fact and opinion

_____ 2. The fewer laws, the better.
   a. fact
   b. opinion
   c. combination of fact and opinion

_____ 3. In Western civilization, the foundation for the explanation of criminal behavior is rooted in the religious beliefs of the European Middle Ages and the Renaissance.
   a. fact
   b. opinion
   c. combination of fact and opinion

_____ 4. In 1932, 25 percent of the labor force was out of work in the United States.
   a. fact
   b. opinion
   c. combination of fact and opinion

_____ 5. The Gulf War led to a reshaping of the Middle East's political map.
   a. fact
   b. opinion
   c. combination of fact and opinion

B. Directions: Read the paragraph and answer the questions that follow.

[1]In many animal species the female gives off a scent that *draws* males, often from far distances, and thus ensures the continuation of the species. [2]Humans, too, emit sexual *attractants* called sex pheromones, body secretions that arouse sexual desire. [3]Humans, of course, supplement that with perfumes, colognes, after-shave lotions, powders, and the like to further enhance attractiveness and sexuality. [4]Not surprisingly, biotechnology companies are busily at work with the aim of bottling human sex pheromones. [5]Women, recent research finds, prefer the scent of men who bear a close genetic similarity to themselves, a finding that may account, in part, for our attraction to people much like ourselves.

—DeVito, *The Interpersonal Communication Book*, 10th ed., p. 205.

_____ 6. Sentence 1 is an example of _____.
   a. fact
   b. opinion
   c. combination of fact and opinion

_____ 7. Sentence 2 is an example of _____.
   a. fact
   b. opinion
   c. combination of fact and opinion

_____ 8. Sentence 3 is an example of _____.
   a. fact
   b. opinion
   c. combination of fact and opinion

_____ 9. Sentence 4 is an example of _____.
   a. fact
   b. opinion
   c. combination of fact and opinion

_____ 10. Sentence 5 is an example of _____.
   a. fact
   b. opinion
   c. combination of fact and opinion

Name_____Section_____Date_____Score (number correct) _____ x 10 = _____

A. Directions: Read the statements and decide if they are facts, opinions, or a combination of fact and opinion.

_____ 1. The Catholic Church was the major source of criminal law during Europe's Middle Ages, and the Church was an active agent in determining the guilt or innocence of individuals accused of breaking the law.
a. fact
b. opinion
c. combination of fact and opinion

_____ 2. In the American colonies, the infamous Salem witch trials of 1692 are a testament to the extent to which people believed in evil spirits, supernatural explanations, and a cosmic battle of good against evil.
a. fact
b. opinion
c. combination of fact and opinion

_____ 3. Between 1672 and 1692, there were 40 cases filed involving the Devil in the Massachusetts Bay Colony.
a. fact
b. opinion
c. combination of fact and opinion

_____ 4. During the time of the Salem Witch trials, any unusual event in one of the colonies was attributed to mystical powers, including coincidences, unusual diseases, and misfortunes.
a. fact
b. opinion
c. combination of fact and opinion

_____ 5. During the height of the witchcraft trials in 1692, over 150 people were arrested, 19 people were hanged for practicing witchcraft, one was pressed to death, and four died while in prison awaiting trial.
a. fact
b. opinion
c. combination of fact and opinion

_____ 6. Drug use among adolescents has decreased during the past five years.
a. fact
b. opinion
c. combination of fact and opinion

B. Directions: Read the following paragraph and answer the questions that follow.

Learning Readiness. [1]Researcher Eric Lenneberg (1921–1975) claimed that human beings are born with a grammatical capacity and a readiness to produce language. [2]Lenneberg believed that the brain continues to develop from birth until about age 13, with the greatest development leap taking place around age two. [3]During this period, children develop grammar and learn the rules of language. [4]After age 13, there is little room for improvement or change in an individual's neurological structure. [5]Lenneberg supported his argument with the observation that brain-damaged children can relearn some speech and language, whereas brain-damaged adolescents or adults who lose language and speech are unable to regain the lost ability completely. [6]Lenneberg's view is persuasive, but some of his original claims have been seriously criticized—particularly his idea of the role of a critical time period in language development, although this is shown to be the case in some animals, such as birds and fish.

[7]Some researchers claim that not only human beings but also other animals—for example, chimpanzees—are born with a grammatical capacity and a readiness for language.

—Adapted from Lefton and Brannon, *Psychology,* 8th ed., p. 325

_____ 7. Lenneberg's claim that human beings are born with a grammatical capacity and readiness to produce language represents _____.
  a. fact
  b. informed opinion
  c. expert opinion

_____ 8. Lenneberg's belief that the brain continues to develop from birth until about age 13, with the greatest development leap taking place around age two is _____.
  a. fact
  b. informed opinion
  c. expert opinion

_____ 9. Sentence 3 is an example of _____.
  a. fact
  b. opinion
  c. a combination of fact and opinion

_____ 10. Lenneberg's argument is supported by _____.
  a. fact
  b. informed opinion
  c. expert opinion

Chapter 10: Tone and Purpose
LAB 10.1 PRACTICE EXERCISE 1

Name_____ Section _____ Date _____ Score (number correct) _____ x 10 = _____

A. Directions: Read the paragraphs and answer the questions that follow.

Hebrews, Israelites, and Jews

[1]The people who wrote and collected the books of the Old Testament, the offspring of the Patriarchs, are known variously as Hebrews, Israelites, and Jews. [2]They began as an identifiable group around 1200 B.C.E., and they described themselves as both a religious and a national entity. [3]The word *Hebrew*, as we note momentarily, refers to Abraham's ethnic group. [4]Eventually Abraham's descendents came to be called *Israel* (after Abraham's grandson). [5]Around 922 B. C. E., the kingdom of Israel divided and the Northern Kingdom was destroyed. [6]When Babylon destroyed the surviving Southern Kingdom, Judah (named for its major tribe), in 587 B. C.E., the people of the nation of Judah were taken into captivity in Babylon. [7]Later, the expression of Israelite religion became known as Judaism, from which came the words *Jew* and *Jewish*, meaning followers of Judaism and/or members of the ethnic group from which Judaism originated.

[8]The ancestors of Israel were semi-nomadic peoples from Mesopotamia. [9]The Israelites traced their history back to a patriarch named Abram (later Abraham) who lived in "Ur of the Chaldees" in the second millennium B.C.E. [10]According to biblical tradition (Genesis/Exodus), Abram took his wife and household from the heathen environment of Haran and traveled to Canaan. [11]Canaan held a particular spiritual appeal to Abram, because he believed that the land there was suitable for the fulfillment of a destiny to which he had been appointed by God. [12]Canaan was a secluded hill country, which made it possible for Abram and his people to practice their religion in relative peace and isolation. [13]On the other hand, Canaan lay quite close to important trade routes of the ancient world and was thus in a good position for spreading the new religion. [14]Because they came from the other side of the Euphrates, Abram and his family were known as Hebrews, from a word meaning "the other side." [15]Abram had a son, Isaac, through whose line of descent God's promises were seen to continue. [16]As a boy, Isaac was nearly sacrificed by Abram at God's command (Genesis, chapter 22).

—Adapted from Sporre, *The Creative Impulse*, 6th ed., pp. 144–45.

_____1. The primary purpose of this passage is _____.
    a. to explain the origin of the Hebrews, Israelites, and Jews
    b. to persuade the reader to acknowledge the importance of Hebrews, Israelites, and Jews.
    c. to entertain the reader with mythical details about the culture of the Hebrews, Israelites, and Jews.

_____2. The tone of the sentences 1 through 3 is _____.
    a. informal
    b. academic
    c. confident
    d. sad

_____3. The tone of sentence 9 is _____.
   a. informal
   b. factual
   c. humorous
   d. poetic

_____4. The tone of sentence 10 is _____.
   a. critical
   b. cynical
   c. objective
   d. subjective

_____5. The purpose of the information stated in sentence 16 is _____.
   a. to inform the reader about Abram's level of devotion and obedience to God
   b. to persuade the reader that Abram's God is a cruel God who required a human sacrifice
   c. to entertain the reader with a vivid detail about Abram and his relationship with his God

B. Directions: Label each type of writing according to its purpose.

_____6. The classified section of the newspaper
   a. to inform
   b. to persuade
   c. to entertain

_____7. A mystery novel
   a. to inform
   b. to persuade
   c. to entertain

_____8. A television commercial
   a. to inform
   b. to persuade
   c. to entertain

_____9. A medical advice column in a magazine
   a. to inform
   b. to persuade
   c. to entertain

_____10. An anti-smoking poster
   a. to inform
   b. to persuade
   c. to entertain

Name_____ Section _____ Date _____ Score (number correct) _____ x 10 = _____

Objective: To identify an author's tone and purpose.

A. Directions: Read the paragraph and answer the questions that follow.

Aristotle (384–322 B.C.) and the Greeks were the first to articulate the notion of **natural law**, the doctrine that human affairs should be governed by certain ethical principles. In the thirteenth century, the Italian priest and philosopher Thomas Aquinas (1225–1274) gave the idea of natural law a new, Christian framework. He argued that natural law and Christianity were compatible because God created the natural law that established individual rights to life and liberty. In contradiction to this view, kings throughout Europe continued to rule as absolute monarchs, claiming this divine right came directly from God.

—O'Connor and Sabato, *The Essentials of American Government*, 3rd ed., pp. 5–6

____ 1. Which term best describes the tone of the first sentence?
   a. academic
   b. informal
   c. argumentative
   d. humorous

____ 2. The tone of this paragraph can be described as _____.
   a. objective
   b. subjective
   c. optimistic
   d. discouraged

____ 3. The primary purpose of this paragraph is to _____.
   a. to persuade the reader to agree with Thomas Aquinas
   b. to entertain the reader with a historical antidote
   c. to inform the reader about the doctrine of natural law

[1]One of the essential qualities of living things is that they grow and reproduce. [2]Both growth and reproduction depend heavily on **cell division**, the process by which one cell gives rise to two or more cells. [3]The process is organized such that a parent cell accurately distributes both genes and other cell components to its daughter cells. [4]In eukaryotes, there are two types of cell division: mitotic and meiotic. [5]**Mitotic cell division** yields daughter cells that are genetically identical to the original cell. [6]In **meiotic cell division** the daughter cells are not genetically identical to each other or to the original cell.

—Audersirk, Audersirk, and Byers, *Life on Earth*, 3rd ed., p. 139

____ 4. Which term best describes the tone of sentence 2?
   a. poetic
   b. informal
   c. scientific
   d. light

____ 5. The tone of this paragraph can be described as _____.
   a. biased
   b. disappointed
   c. unbiased
   d. demoralizing

____ 6. The primary purpose of this paragraph is to _____.
   a. to persuade the reader that scientific work is important
   b. to entertain the reader with an episode from a scientific journal
   c. to inform the reader about the process of cell division

When I first arrived in Morocco, I found the sights that greeted me exotic—not far removed from my memories of *Casablanca, Raiders of the Lost Ark*, and other movies that over the years had become part of my collective memory.

—Henslin, *The Essentials of Sociology*, 5th ed., p. 33

____ 7. The tone of the word *exotic* is _____.
   a. mocking and critical
   b. argumentative and angry
   c. technical and complicated
   d. unusual and intriguing

____ 8. The tone of the sentence is _____.
   a. disgruntled
   b. amazed
   c. unimpressed
   d. objective

____ 9. This sentence can be described as _____.
   a. objective
   b. subjective
   c. formal
   d. academic

___ 10. The primary purpose of this passage is to _____.
   a. to persuade the reader to visit Morocco
   b. to entertain the reader with memories of old movies
   c. to inform the reader about the exciting and unusual sights in Morocco

Name_____ Section _____ Date _____ Score (number correct) _____ x 10 = _____

A. Directions: Read the paragraphs and answer the questions that follow.

[1]A year after his election to the presidency, Jimmy Carter told a reporter that ". . . it's a strange thing that you can go through your campaign for president, and you have a basic theme that you express in a 15- or 20- minute standard speech, . . . but the traveling press—sometimes exceeding 100 people—will never report that speech to the public. [2]The peripheral aspects become the headlines, but the basic essence of what you stand for and what you hope to accomplish is never reported."

—Edwards, Wattenberg, and Lineberry, *Government in America*, 9th ed., p. 230

_____ 1. The tone of sentence 2 is _____.
    a. objective
    b. subjective
    c. formal
    d. academic

_____ 2. The tone of the passage is _____.
    a. delighted
    b. cheerful
    c. apathetic
    d. frustrated

_____ 3. The primary purpose of this paragraph is to _____.
    a. to persuade the reader that the press is dishonest in its treatment of presidential candidates
    b. to entertain the reader with an hilarious story of the presidential campaign trail
    c. to inform the reader of Carter's annoyance over press reports that seem to focus on extraneous details rather than the contents of his campaign speech

[1]Rather than presenting their audience with the whole chicken, the media typically give just a McNugget. [2]Why should politicians work to build a carefully crafted case for their point of view when a catchy line will do just as well?

—Edwards, Wattenberg, and Lineberry, *Government in America*, 9th ed., p. 230

_____ 4. The tone of the words *chicken* and *McNugget* in sentence 1 is _____?
    a. sarcastic
    b. angry
    c. technical
    d. authoritative

_____ 5. The tone of this passage is _____.
    a. insensitive
    b. objective
    c. critical
    d. cheerful

_____ 6. The primary purpose of this paragraph is to _____.
    a. to persuade the reader that Chicken McNuggets are good food choices.
    b. to entertain the reader with an amusing story of how the media gives McNuggets
    c. to inform the reader that the media often influences a politician's speeches

[1]While few equate immorality with criminality, the similarities are striking. [2]First, moral codes and laws are linguistically expressed, often employing words such as *shall* and *shall not.* [3]Second, at the heart of both concepts is the idea of intentionality, meaning that it is reasonable to hold people both morally and legally responsible for behavior that they intended to happen. [4]Third, most believe that it is appropriate to punish people who violate both moral codes and criminal statutes, unless those people happen to be very young. [5]Finally, there is considerable overlap between the acts that are considered criminal.

—Ellis & Walsh, *Criminology,* pp. 313–14

_____ 7. The tone of the word *shall* and *shall not* in sentence 2 is _____?
    a. critical
    b. insincere
    c. vague
    d. unconditional

_____ 8. Which term best describes the tone of sentence 1?
    a. academic
    b. informal
    c. apathetic
    d. cold

_____ 9. The tone of this paragraph can be described as _____.
    a. emotional
    b. neutral
    c. disbelieving
    d. ironic

_____ 10. The primary purpose of this paragraph is to _____.
    a. illustrate the point that criminality and morality have some common grounds for comparison
    b. entertain the reader with a personal experience of punishment for breaking the law
    c. inform the reader of the laws concerning punishment for criminal behavior

Chapter 10: Tone and Purpose
LAB 10.4 REVIEW TEST 2

Name_____ Section _____ Date _____ Score (number correct) _____ x 10 = _____

Directions: Read the paragraphs and answer the questions that follow.

[1]There's only one thing that can slay the hunger of a young guy on the move: the Thickburger line at Hardee's. [2]With nine cravable varieties, including the classic Original Thickburger and the monument to decadence, the Monster Thickburger, quick-service goes premium with 100% Angus beef and all the fixings. . . . [3]If you want to indulge in a big, delicious, juicy burger, look no further than Hardee's.

—Adapted from Kotler and Armstrong, *Principles of Marketing*, 13th ed., p. 589.

_____1. The tone of the words *monument to decadence* and *indulge* in sentences 2 and 3 is _____.
   a. neutral
   b. unbiased
   c. critical
   d. admiring

_____2. The primary purpose of this paragraph is _____.
   a. to entertain the reader with a humorous story of a young man who is addicted to Hardee's Thickburgers.
   b. To inform the reader of the special quality of Hardee's Thickburgers
   c. To persuade the reader eat at Hardees.

_____3. The tone of this paragraph is _____.
   a. anxious
   b. critical
   c. grave
   d. complimentary

[1]At a time when other fast-food chains such as McDonald's, Wendys, and Subway were getting "leaner," Hardee's introduced the decadent Thickburger, featuring a third of a pound of Angus beef. [2]It followed up with the Monster Thickburger: two-thirds of a pound of Angus beef, four strips of bacon, and three slices of American cheese, all nestled in a buttered sesame-seed bun slathered with mayonnaise. [3]The Monster Thickburger weighs in at a whopping 1,410 calories and 107 grams of fat, far greater than the government's recommended fat intake for an entire day. [4]Is Hardee's being socially irresponsible by aggressively promoting overindulgence to ill-informed or unwary consumers?

—Adapted from Kotler and Armstrong, *Principles of Marketing*, 13th ed., p. 589.

_____4. The tone of the words *slathered* and *whopping* in sentences 2 and 3 is _____.
   a. respectful
   b. unbiased
   c. condemning
   d. admiring

_____ 5. The primary purpose of this paragraph is _____.
   a. to amuse the reader with a humorous story of a young man who is addicted to Hardee's Thickburgers.
   b. to inform the reader of the delicious hamburger choices at Hardee's
   c. to suggest to reader that Hardee's is promoting over-indulgence in a socially irresponsible way.

_____ 6. The tone of this paragraph is _____.
   a. light
   b. critical
   c. grave
   d. complimentary

[1]Scott Adams, creator of the *Dilbert* comic strip, first worked at Crocker Bank in San Francisco, and then at Pacific Bell. [2]It was there, in 1989, that he began drawing Dilbert, a mouthless engineer with a perpetually bent necktie. [3]Adams says he won't reveal his actual earnings from *Dilbert*, because, as he says, "My family might expect better gifts from me." [4]In one comic strip, Dilbert was consulting with a financial advisor who was pushing his firm's "churn 'n 'burn" family of mutual funds. [5]"We'll turn your worthless equity into valuable brokerage fees in just three days!" the advisor raved. [6]In another strip, Dogbert, Dilbert's potato-shaped dog and companion, set himself up as a financial consultant and announced, "I'll tell all my clients to invest in the 'Dogbert Deferred Earnings Fund.'"
[7]"Isn't that a conflict of interest?" Dilbert asks.
[8]"Only if I show interest in the client," replies Dogbert.

   —Adapted from Keown, *Personal Finance: Turning Money into Wealth*, 5th ed., pp. 468-469.

_____ 7. The tone of sentences 1 and 2 is _____.
   a. factual
   b. biased
   c. negative
   d. positive

_____ 8. The tone of the phrase "*My family might expect better gifts from me*" is one of _____.
   a. complaining
   b. anxious
   c. critical
   d. humorous

_____ 9. The tone of this selection is _____.
   a. disgruntled
   b. argumentative
   c. humorous
   d. angry

_____ 10. The primary purpose of this paragraph is _____.
   a. to inform the reader about the origin of the cartoon *Dilbert*
   b. to amuse the reader with some entertaining examples from *Dilbert* that mock the financial world
   c. to persuade the reader that Dilbert is one of the greatest cartoons that will offer hilarious entertainment every week.

Chapter 10: Tone and Purpose
LAB 10.5 MASTERY TEST 1

Name _____ Section _____ Date _____ Score (number correct) _____ x 10 = _____

A. Directions: Read the passages and answer the questions that follow.

A year after the birth of their first child, Sharese and Ernie received a phone call from Heather, who asked how well they liked parenthood: "Is it a joy, a dilemma, a stressful experience-how would you describe it?"
Chuckling, Sharese and Ernie responded in unison, "All of the above!"

—Berk, Development Through the Lifespan, 3rd ed., p. 463

_____ 1. The tone of this passage can be described as _____.
    a. timid
    b. humorous
    c. impartial
    d. doubtful

_____ 2. The primary purpose of this passage is to _____.
    a. to persuade the reader that parenthood is quite demanding and not for everyone
    b. to entertain the reader with a personal glimpse into parenthood
    c. to illustrate the need for parenting classes

[1]Whether love is defined as the sweetest thing, whether it makes the world go 'round, or whether as the song claims, it's all you need, a popular belief is that love is as important as breathable air. [2]Even the high divorce rate has not interfered with the belief that living alone is unnatural or that there is no happiness outside commitment to one other person. [3]A first "mistake" requires the search for the right choice next time, and a newly single person's claim of being happy is met with disbelief and offers of matchmaking. [4]The myth is not only that there is someone for everyone but that love and talk of love can substitute for every other human attribute.

—Janaro and Altshuler, *The Art of Being Human*, 7th ed., p. 75

_____ 3. The tone of sentence 1 is _____.
    a. bitter
    b. scoffing
    c. bored
    d. approving

_____ 4. The tone of this paragraph can be described as _____.
    a. doubtful
    b. sad
    c. jovial
_____   d. encouraging

_____ 5. The primary purpose of this paragraph is to _____.
    a. persuade the reader that a love relationship is not a absolutely necessary to a fulfilling life
    b. entertain the reader with romantic lyrics from popular songs
    c. inform the reader of the necessity of picking a partner very carefully

B. Directions: Read the poem by Judith Viorst and answer the questions that follow.

. . . And Although the Little Mermaid Sacrificed Everything to Win the Love of the Prince, the Prince (Alas) Decided to Wed Another

I left the castle of my mer-king father,   *1*
Where seaweed gardens sway in pearly sand.
I left behind sweet sisters and kind waters
To seek a prince's love upon the land.
My tongue was payment for the witch's potion   *2*
(And never would I sing sea songs again).
My tail became two human legs to dance on,
But I would always dance with blood and pain.
I risked more than my life to make him love me.   *3*
The prince preferred another for his bride.
I always hate the ending to this story:
They lived together happily; I died.
But I have some advice for modern mermaids   *4*
Who wish to save great sorrow and travail:
Don't give up who you are for love of princes.
He might have liked me better with my tail.

Viorst, *If I Were in Charge of the World*, 1981, pp. 30–31

_____ 6. The purpose of the title is _____.
   a. to persuade the reader to locate a copy of the original Hans Christian Andersen tale "The Little Mermaid."
   b. to inform the reader that what follows is a commentary on the rest of the Hans Christian Andersen tale.
   c. to entertain the reader with the happy ending of the film adaptation of "The Little Mermaid."
   d. to entertain the reader with a better ending to the original Hans Christian Andersen story.

_____ 7. The speaker of the poem is _____.
   a. The mer-king
   b. The mermaid's sister
   c. The witch
   d. The Little Mermaid

_____ 8. The purpose of stanza 1 is _____.
   a. to persuade the reader to compare her description of home to that of the reader's
   b. to persuade the reader to help her escape her unfortunate choice
   c. to entertain the reader with images from her new life
   d. to inform the reader about the differences between her new life and the one she had hoped to have

____ 9. The purpose of stanza 3 is _____.
   a. To persuade the reader to take her side in the story
   b. To inform the reader about the bitter ending to her story
   c. To persuade the poet to rewrite the ending to be more pleasing to other readers
   d. To entertain the reader with a happy scene

___ 10. The purpose of stanza 4 is _____.
   a. To inform the reader that the prince is her husband, but she is not happy with him
   b. To entertain the reader with a humorous view of her mortal husband
   c. To entertain the reader with a sneak preview at what life is like after the wedding
   d. To persuade readers to be true to themselves rather than trying to accommodate the apparent wishes of a potential mate

Chapter 10: Tone and Purpose
LAB 10.6 MASTERY TEST 2

Name _____ Section _____ Date _____ Score (number correct) _____ x 10 = _____

Directions: Read the passages and answer the questions that follow.

The Family as a System

[1]*We live our lives like chips in a kaleidoscope, always a part of patterns that are larger than ourselves and somehow more than the sum of their parts.*
—Salvador Minuchin, *Family Kaleidoscope*

[2]When individuals come together to form relationships, what is created is larger and more complex than the sum of the individuals; what is created is a system. [3]When individuals form families, they also create family systems built on their interaction patterns. [4]Taking a systems perspective provides valuable insights into a family's communication patterns. [5]Because communication is a symbolic and transactional process, focus must be placed on family relationships, not on individual members. [6]In order to understand the communication patterns of family members, the overall communication context—the family system— must be examined.

[7]The following personal statement provides insight into how a family operates systemically and reflects the complexity of the task of examining families from a systems perspective.

[8]Family life is incredibly subtle and complex. [9]Everything seems tied to everything else, and it's very difficult to sort out what is going on. [10]For example, when our oldest daughter, Marcy, contracted spinal meningitis, the whole family reflected the strain. [11]My second daughter and I fought more, while my husband tended to withdraw into himself, which brought me closer to my son. [12]In their own ways, the three children became close while our marriage became more distant. [13]As Marcy's recovery progressed, there were more changes which affected how we relate now, two years later. [14]That one event highlighted the difficulty of sorting out what is really going on within our family.

—Adapted from Galvin and Brommel, *Family Communication:
Cohesion and Change*, 5th ed., pp. 50–51

_____ 1. Which word best describes the tone of the quote that opens the passage?
    a. detached
    b. poetic
    c. respectful
    d. confused

_____ 2. The tone of the first and second paragraphs (sentences 2 through 7) is _____.
    a. scholarly
    b. conversational
    c. boring
    d. haughty

_____ 3. The purpose of the third paragraph (sentences 8 – 14) is _____.
   a. to entertain the reader with a personal story
   b. to use a personal story to illustrate the complexity of a family system
   c. to prove how difficult life is for many families

_____ 4. Which word best describes the tone of the third paragraph?
   a. subjective
   b. objective
   c. unbiased
   d. dispassionate

_____ 5. The use of the first person (*my* and *our*) to relate one family's story in the third paragraph provides a tone that is _____.
   a. detached
   b. impersonal
   c. personal
   d. unbiased

_____ 6. The overall purpose of this passage is _____.
   a. to inform
   b. to persuade
   c. to entertain

[1]College is a critical time to become aware of and responsible for drinking. [2]There is little doubt that drinking is a part of campus culture and tradition. [3]Many students are away from home, often for the first time, and are excited by their new found independence. [4]For some students, this independence and the rite of passage into the college culture are symbolized by the use of alcohol. [5]It provides the answer to one of the most commonly heard statements on any college campus: "There is nothing to do." [6]Additionally, many students say they drink to have fun. [7]Having fun, which often means drinking simply to get drunk, may really be a way of coping with stress, boredom, anxiety, or pressures created by academic and social demands.

[8]Some students even indulge in binge drinking. [9]The stakes of binge drinking are high because it poses high risk for alcohol-related injuries and death. [10]According to a recent study, 1,700 college students die each year because of alcohol-related, unintentional injuries, including car accidents. [11]Unfortunately, binge drinkers cause problems not only for themselves, but also for those around them.

—Adapted from Donatelle, *Health: the Basics*, 8th ed., p. 217

_____ 7. The tone of sentence 1 is _____.
   a. insensitive
   b. concerned
   c. critical
   d. chatty

_____ 8. The tone of the quote ("There is nothing to do.") in sentence 5 is _____.
   a. angry
   b. bitter
   c. hostile
   d. bored

___ 9. The purpose of the first paragraph is _____.
   a. to inform the reader about the reasons why college students use alcohol
   b. to persuade college students to stop drinking
   c. to entertain the reader with some of the mishaps of college life

___ 10. The overall tone of this passage is _____.
   a. informative
   b. afraid
   c. fretful
   d. argumentative

Chapter 11: Inferences
LAB 11.1 PRACTICE EXERCISE 1

Name_____ Section _____ Date _____ Score (number correct) _____ x 10 = _____

Objective: To use supporting details to make accurate inferences.

A. Directions: Read the passage below. Decide if the following statements are valid inferences that are firmly based on the information in the passage.

Vian sat in the first seat in the middle row of desks in the classroom. Unlike Jessie, who sat in the last desk in the row next to the door, Vian could see the entire chalkboard and the multimedia screen. Vian read the textbook assignments before class but had several questions, which she asked throughout the class period. Every time Vian asked a question, Jessie rolled her eyes and shifted in her seat impatiently. Vian took careful notes; Jessie took no notes. After class, several students thanked Vian for asking questions, stating that they had the same needs for clarification.

_____1. Most of the students in the class are annoyed with Vian for asking so many questions.
    a. valid inference
    b. not a valid inference

_____2. Vian chose her seat so that she could see the information presented in class.
    a. valid inference
    b. not a valid inference

_____3. Vian's interest in asking questions annoyed Jessie.
    a. valid inference
    b. not a valid inference

_____4. Jessie did not ask questions or take notes because she already understood the material.
    a. valid inference
    b. not a valid inference

B. Directions: Read the following passages and determine the most logical inference based on the passages.

Homeowner's Insurance

[1]Homeowner's insurance protects a homeowner against the cost of property damage, theft, or personal liability related to owning a home. [2]For many, it protects their most valuable asset. [3]It also limits some possible liabilities or expenses connected to the home. [4]This insurance is often paid on a yearly basis. [5]Or the cost may be built into your house payments.

[6]Financial loss due to the ownership of a home could occur from a wide variety of adverse events, ranging from flood to burglary. [7]Homeowner's insurance is offered in six different packages, which are based on the degree of coverage. [8]Most homeowner's insurance policies offer the following types of coverage.

[9]A homeowner's insurance policy as a rule provides coverage of property damage to the home. [10]The specific terms of the policy explain the degree of coverage. [11]A cash value policy pays you for the value of the damaged property after allowing for its wear and tear. [12]A replacement cost policy pays you for the

actual cost of replacing the damaged home. [13]The cost of replacing damaged property is usually higher than the assessed value of the property. [14]For example, assume a home is destroyed and was valued at $90,000. [15]A cash value policy offers coverage for $90,000. [16]However, the cost of rebuilding your house could be $100,000 or more. [17]In contrast, the replacement cost policy would pay for the entire cost of repairing the damage up to a limit set out in the policy.

[18]The policy may also cover separate structures such as a garage, a shed, or a swimming pool. [19]Trees and shrubs are usually included up to a stated limit. [20]A policy also often covers personal assets such as furniture, computers, or clothing up to a stated amount. [21]For example, a policy may state that all personal assets are covered up to $40,000. [22]A homeowner should create a home inventory; this list includes detailed information about your personal property. [23]Use a video camera to film your personal assets in your home for proof of their existence. [24]Keep the list and the video in a safe place outside the home, so that you have access to them even if your home is destroyed.

[25]The policy also offers coverage in case you are sued because of an event that occurs on your property. [26]Normally, you are responsible for an injury to another person while they are on your property. [27]For example, if a neighbor falls down the steps of your home and sues you, your policy would likely cover you. [28]Your liability is not tied to the value of your home. [29]Even if you have a small home with a low value, you need to protect against liability. [30]Some insurance companies offer minimum coverage of $100,000 against liability. [31]However, a higher level of coverage, such as $300,000, is often recommended. [32]The coverage includes court costs and awards granted as a result of lawsuits.

[33]There are many other types of terms that could be included in a policy to cover a wide variety of events. [34]For example, if a fire forces you to live away from home, you will face additional living expenses. [35]A loss-of-use provision covers these expenses up to a stated amount.

—Adapted from Madura, *Personal Finance*, 2nd ed., pp. 307–10.

_____5. What inference can the reader make about owning a home?
    a. Owning a home is not worth the risk.
    b. Owning a home is only for the wealthy.
    c. Owning a home entails risks.
    d. Owning a home is a waste of money.

_____6. The reader can infer that the term *liabilities* in sentence 3 probably means _____.
    a. mistakes made by the home owner
    b. assets owned by the home owner
    c. payments made to the insurance company
    d. expenses caused by damage or harm

_____7. The reader can infer that the term *adverse* in sentence 6 probably means _____.
    a. harmful
    b. poor
    c. exciting
    d. unsympathetic

_____8. From sentence 20, the reader can infer that _____.
   a. if your car catches on fire while parked on your property, homeowner's insurance will cover the repair costs
   b. if your computer is damaged by an electrical storm, your policy will pay up to a certain amount to repair or replace it
   c. if you outgrow your clothes, your policy will pay for a new wardrobe
   d. if your furniture is outdated your policy will provide money to replace it

_____9. From sentences 12 and 13, the reader can infer that _____.
   a. A replacement policy costs more than a cash value policy.
   b. A cash value policy is more expensive than a replacement policy.
   c. A replacement policy offers less than the value of the assessed value of the damaged property.
   d. A replacement policy takes into account the age of an item and the wear and tear when determining replacement costs.

_____10. According to the information in the article, a homeowner is not responsible for injuries that occur on his or her property.
   a. This is a valid inference
   b. This is not a valid inference

Chapter 11: Inferences
LAB 11.2 PRACTICE EXERCISE 2

Name _____ Section _____ Date _____ Score (number correct) _____ x 10 = _____

Objective: To use supporting details to make accurate inferences.

A. Directions: Read the poem by Archibald MacLeish, and then answer the questions that follow it.

Ars Poetica

A poem should be palpable and mute   1
As a globed fruit,
Dumb
As old medallions to the thumb,
Silent as the sleeve-worn stone
Of casement ledges where the moss has grown—
A poem should be wordless
As the flight of birds.
A poem should be motionless in time   2
As the moon climbs,
Leaving, as the moon releases
Twig by twig the night-entangled trees,
Leaving, as the moon behind the winter leaves,
Memory by memory the mind—
A poem should be motionless in time
As the moon climbs
A poem should be equal to: 3
Not true.
For all the history of grief
An empty doorway and a maple leaf.
For love
The leaning grasses and two lights above the sea—
A poem should not mean
But be.

   —From *Collected Poems 1917–1982* by Archibald MacLeish, Boston: Houghton Mifflin, 1985.

_____ 1. The reader can infer that the topic of the poem is _____.
   a. the simplicity of poems
   b. the difficulty of understanding poems
   c. the experience of poetry
   d. the boring nature of poetry

_____ 2. The read can infer that the most likely definition of *palpable* in the first line is _____.
   a. present
   b. fragrant
   c. touchable
   d. fleeting

_____ 3. How many comparisons are drawn in the first stanza?
   a. two   b. three   c. four   d. five

_____ 4. Which of the following images does the poet use in the second stanza?
   a. moon and two twigs
   b. deep sea and bright sun
   c. autumn mornings and spring afternoons
   d. winter snows and summer winds

_____ 5. Which statement can the reader conclude is the main idea of the poem?
   a. Poetry is simply the definition of its words.
   b. Poetry is an experience that cannot be reduced to the meaning of its words.
   c. Most poets do not intend deep meaning for their poems, but rely on the reader's interpretation.
   d. All poems seem as illusory as moonlight, but their meanings are written in stone.

B. Directions: Read the paragraph. Decide if the following statements are valid inferences that are firmly based on the information in the sentence.

Studies show that many drugs affect prenatal development. High doses of aspirin, caffeine, or tobacco all have negative effects. Cigarette smoking constricts the oxygen supply to the fetus. Babies born to mothers who smoke cigarettes tend to be smaller and may be at increased risk for cleft palate and perhaps a slightly lower I.Q. Certain drugs, including tranquilizers, can produce malformations of the head, face, and limbs as well as neurological disorders. And, in recent years, hundreds of thousands of infants have been born addicted to crack and other drugs. Drugs may have an especially strong influence during the embryonic stage of development, when the mother may not realize she is pregnant; this is usually considered a critical period.

    —Lefton and Brannon, *Psychology,* 8th ed., pp.77–78.

_____ 6. What a woman ingests in the first month of her pregnancy can affect the embryo.
   a. valid inference
   b. not a valid inference

_____ 7. Drinking coffee while pregnant has more negative effects on a fetus than smoking.
   a. valid inference
   b. not a valid inference

_____ 8. Most drugs, except aspirin, can negatively affect an unborn child.
   a. valid inference
   b. not a valid inference

_____ 9. If a pregnant woman does not smoke, she can use coffee or alcohol in moderation.
   a. valid inference
   b. not a valid inference

_____ 10. Some birth defects can be prevented with good prenatal care.
   a. valid inference
   b. not a valid inference

Chapter 11: Inferences
LAB 11.3 REVIEW TEST 1

Name _____ Section _____ Date _____ Score (number correct) _____ x 10 = _____

Directions: Read the passages below. Decide if the following statements are valid inferences that are firmly based on the information in the passage.

[1]Severe **acute** respiratory syndrome (SARS) is a respiratory illness caused by a virus. [2]SARS first appeared in Southern China in November 2002, and it became a global threat in March 2003. [3]The illness usually has a sudden onset that begins with a high fever. [4]Other symptoms may include chills, headache, a general feeling of discomfort, and body aches. [5]Some people also experience mild respiratory symptoms at first. [6]Diarrhea is seen in about 10 percent to 20 percent of patients. [7]After 2 to 7 days, SARS patients may develop a dry cough. [8]Most patients develop pneumonia. [9]SARS appears to be spread mainly by close person-to-person contact through the coughs and sneezes of an infected person. [10]The virus also can spread when a person touches a contaminated surface or object and then touches his or her mouth, nose, or eye(s).

> —Adapted from "Severe Acute Respiratory Syndrome (SARS)," CDC.13 Feb. 2004.
> http://www.cdc.gov/ncidod/sars/faq.htm

____ 1. The word *acute* in sentence 1 means "mild."
   a. valid inference
   b. not a valid inference

____ 2. Diarrhea is a main indicator of this illness.
   a. valid inference
   b. not a valid inference

____ 3. Everyone who comes down with SARS will develop pneumonia.
   a. valid inference
   b. not a valid inference

____ 4. Washing hands frequently could help control the spread of SARS.
   a. valid inference
   b. not a valid inference

____ 5. SARS is a disease that has resulted from the misuse of biological weapons.
   a. valid inference
   b. not a valid inference

Thought Stopping

[1]Thought stopping is a technique whereby an individual intentionally breaks the anxious cycle by abruptly leaving the **obsessive** thoughts. [2]This can be done by two different methods. [3]The more traditional technique of thought stopping involves shouting "STOP!" as soon as you become aware of anxious thoughts. [4]At first the word may be shouted to yourself. [5]If this is not forceful enough, shouting it out loud will successfully destroy the anxious cycle. [6]You may then attend to other less-stressful thoughts. [7]Another form of thought stopping is to switch abruptly to a pleasing, relaxing image or scene in your "mind's eye" as soon as you become aware of the anxious cycle. [8]The scene should be the same one each

155

time and should be a place, real or imagined, that you find aesthetically pleasing and relaxing. [9]After dwelling on this place for thirty to sixty seconds, slowly reoccupy your mind with real-world demands. [10]If no such relaxing image exists for you, counting backward from five to one will also work. [11]Simply picture the numbers in your mind as large and bright images. [12]By the time one is reached, the cycle will be broken, and you can begin thinking of other thoughts. [13]If the cycle starts again, break it in the same manner. [14]Continue doing so until the cycle remains broken, no matter how many thought-stopping maneuvers are necessary.

—Girdano, Everly, and Dusek, *Controlling Stress and Tension,* 6th ed., p. 100.

_____ 6. Based on the overall passage, the word *obsessive* in sentence 1 implies "habitual."
   a. valid inference
   b. not a valid inference

_____ 7. Thought stopping involves replacing one habit with another.
   a. valid inference
   b. not a valid inference

_____ 8. Everyone experiences obsessive, anxious thought cycles at some point in his or her life.
   a. valid inference
   b. not a valid inference

_____ 9. Shouting "STOP!" is the most effective method of breaking the anxious cycle.
   a. valid inference
   b. not a valid inference

_____ 10. Obsessive thinking can be difficult to control.
   a. valid inference
   b. not a valid inference

Name_____Section _____ Date _____ Score (number correct) _____ x 10 = _____

Directions: Read the passages below, then decide if the statements following are valid inferences that are firmly based on the information in the passage.

During Monday night football, Camille told Jared that her boss had invited them to his house Saturday night and that she had accepted the invitation. Jared never took his eyes off the football game as he nodded his head. Saturday morning, Camille reminded Jared of the commitment. Jared replied that he couldn't go because he had promised to help his best friend move. Camille's voice shook as she said, "You have to go with me. It's my boss!" Jared's voice rose to a shout as he replied, "You should have told me sooner." Tears stung Camille's eyes as she said, "This is so typical. You never listen to me."

_____1. Jared and Camille are married.
   a. valid inference
   b. not a valid inference

_____2. Jared and Camille have trouble communicating with each other.
   a. valid inference
   b. not a valid inference

_____3. Jared was paying more attention to the football game than to what Camille told him.
   a. valid inference
   b. not a valid inference

_____4. Jared never listens to Camille.
   a. valid inference
   b. not a valid inference

Suzy studies hard, and her grades show it. But she is also a very tense person and enjoys relaxing by smoking marijuana. Suzy started smoking cigarettes when she was in high school, so smoking marijuana was an easy move for her.

After studying the night before an exam, she smoked a couple of joints with some friends. The next day, Suzy remembered very little of what she had reviewed. She rationalized that she hadn't studied enough—after all, she did take some time off to be with friends.

Even though he studies a lot, James is not a top student. He has to work hard to get B's and C's. So James takes all of his exams seriously. He reviews his class notes ahead of time—not just the night before an exam. And he goes over review questions with his classmates to help him feel more confident when answering the real test questions.

James knows that all work and no play isn't a healthy balance, so, like Suzy, he took some time the night before the exam to be with friends. But he didn't want to cloud his judgment and be fuzzy about facts and concepts during the exam, so he steered clear of friends who smoke pot and hung out with friends who relax in a drug-free way.

—Pruitt and Stein, *Health Styles*, 2nd ed., p. 232.

_____5.   Suzy may not understand all the effects of smoking marijuana.
     a.   valid inference
     b.   not a valid inference

_____6.   Suzy is a frequent marijuana user.
     a.   valid inference
     b.   not a valid inference

_____7.   Marijuana use may affect short-term memory.
     a.   valid inference
     b.   not a valid inference

_____8.   James never smokes marijuana.
     a.   valid inference
     b.   not a valid inference

_____9.   James' choices about how to prepare for the exam were wiser than Suzy's.
     a.   valid inference
     b.   not a valid inference

_____10.   James probably performed better on the test than Suzy did.
     a.   valid inference
     b.   not a valid inference

Name_____ Section _____ Date _____ Score (number correct) _____ x 10 = _____

A. Directions: Read the passage below. Decide if the following statements are valid inferences that are firmly based on the information in the passage.

Complex carbohydrates are made up of sugar, starches, and fibers. Examples include pasta, rice, breads, cereals, beans, and peas. Simple carbohydrates consist mainly of sugar. Simple carbohydrates are found naturally in fruits, some vegetables, and milk. They are also found in processed foods such as cookies, candy, soft drinks and pastries. Complex carbohydrates are often richer in vitamins, minerals, and fiber. Simple carbohydrates in processed foods are high in sugar and calories but low in nutrients. Fresh fruits are healthy simple carbohydrates. Carbohydrates are divided into two basic groups. Most Americans consume too many unhealthy simple carbohydrates, such as cookies, candy, soft drinks, and pastries. Complex carbohydrates are always the better choice of food than simple carbohydrates.

_____ 1. Fresh fruits are healthy complex carbohydrates.
    a. valid inference
    b. not a valid inference

_____ 2. Carbohydrates are divided into many groups.
    a. valid inference
    b. not a valid inference

_____ 3. Most Americans consume too many unhealthy simple carbohydrates, such as cookies, candy, soft drinks, and pastries.
    a. valid inference
    b. not a valid inference

_____ 4. Complex carbohydrates are always the better choice of food than simple carbohydrates.
    a. valid inference
    b. not a valid inference

_____ 5. In a low-carbohydrate diet, a person probably would not eat much sugar.
    a. valid inference
    b. not a valid inference

B. Directions: Read these lines from a poem by Walt Whitman (1819–1892), and then answer the questions that follow.

[1]Have you reckon'd a thousand acres much? have you reckon'd
the earth much?
[2]Have you practis'd so long to learn to read?
[3]Have you felt so proud to get at the meaning of poems?

⁴Stop this day and night with me and you shall possess the origin
of all poems,
⁵You shall possess the good of the earth and sun—(there are millions
of suns left;)
⁶You shall no longer take things at second or third hand, nor look
through the eyes of the dead, nor feed on the specters in books;
⁷You shall not look through my eyes either, nor takes things from me:
⁸You shall listen to all sides and filter them from your self.

—From "Song of Myself," ll. 22–29, *Leaves of Grass* by Walt Whitman. New York: W.W. Norton, 1973.

_____ 6. What definitions of *reckon'd* (reckoned) can be applied to line 1?
     a. ignored and reached
     b. calculated and pondered
     c. plowed and wandered
     d. sowed and planted

_____ 7. Lines 2 and 3 imply that _____.
     a. learning to read well and to understand poetry can take time and practice, but the results are gratifying
     b. learning to read well and to understand poetry comes easily to most people
     c. The speaker is a coach blaming his players for not trying hard enough
     d. The speaker is a farmer expecting his workers to try harder

_____ 8. By "there are millions of suns left," the poet implies there are _____.
     a. many days left
     b. many suns out in the universe to consider
     c. many things to learn still
     d. all of the listed meanings

_____ 9. In the phrase "nor feed on the spectres of books," the word *spectres* is the British spelling of *specters*, which most likely means _____.
     a. examinations
     b. ghosts or objects of dread
     c. generals and guides
     d. writers

_____ 10. From this excerpt of the poem, the reader can infer that it is important _____.
     a. to develop the skills to think for yourself rather than rely on others to tell you how to think
     b. to trust your teachers to give you the answers
     c. to enjoy nature before it is destroyed by humans
     d. to recognize the power of nature and its ability to destroy what humans have made

Name_____ Section _____ Date _____ Score (number correct) _____ x 10 = _____

A. Directions: Read the passage below. Decide if the following statements are valid inferences that are firmly based on the information in the passage.

Case Study: Food Fight

1 The spring sun shines brightly on the Mississippi countryside as a tractor crawls slowly across a field. A farmer is planting his soybean crop. But some critics see the farmer's seemingly harmless activity as extremely dangerous. In this view, the farmer's activity threatens our health, our food supply, and the environment. According to writer Jeremy Rifkin, the farmer and others like him are "spreading chaos throughout the biological world, drowning out the ancient language of creation." Around the world, impassioned protestors demand protection from the farmer's crops.

2 Why does something as ordinary as farming inspire such intense opposition? Because more and more farmers are growing genetically altered, bio-engineered crops. These genetically modified foods have been singled out for especially harsh attack by critics of biotechnology, in part because, unlike most nonagricultural applications of biotechnology, genetic engineering in agriculture is already widespread and common; its products are used by farmers everywhere. You've almost certainly consumed a bioengineered food; such foods are widely sold in the United States and no law requires that they be specially labeled.

3 Agricultural biotechnology is based on the introduction of foreign genes into crop plants. The purpose of such gene transfers is often to confer resistance to a disease, pest, or herbicide. For example, farmers are now planting corn, cotton, and potatoes that contain a gene that helps the plants repel insect pests, reducing the farmers' need to apply pesticides. New, bio-engineered strains of squash, potatoes, and tomatoes resist infection by viral diseases. Cotton, corn, soybeans, and sugar beets have been altered so that they are resistant to particular herbicides; farmers who grow these altered plants can use the herbicides to control weeds without worrying that the herbicides will kill the crops. Other fruits, vegetables, and even farm animals have been genetically engineered for improved yields, better nutritive value, or better resistance to the stress of shipping and handling.

4 The genes that are used to confer desirable qualities on crops are typically drawn from fungi or bacteria.

—Audersirk, Andersirk, and Byers, *Life on Earth*, 3rd ed., p. 187.

_____ 1. From the sentence, "According to writer Jeremy Rifkin, the farmer and others like him are 'spreading chaos throughout the biological world, drowning out the ancient language of creation.'" The reader can conclude that bioengineering _____.
   a. is meeting with criticism from people who see it as extremely dangerous
   b. involves farming technology that few people actually use
   c. is not yet being used
   d. is no longer being used

____ 2. Which is *not* a detail from paragraph 2 that would help the reader conclude why critics are condemning bioengineering?
   a. More and more farmers are growing genetically altered, bioengineered crops.
   b. Genetic engineering in agriculture is already widespread and common.
   c. No law requires that genetically engineered products be specially labeled.
   d. Genetic engineering in agriculture is not yet widespread, but will be in the near future.

____ 3. The author *suggests* that bioengineering is already being done for all of the following reasons *except* _____.
   a. resistance to viral diseases, particular herbicides, and the stress of shipping and handling
   b. improved yields
   c. resistance to extreme temperatures
   d. better nutritive value

____ 4. Genes that are used to provide desirable traits in crops are typically drawn from _____.
   a. pesticides
   b. fungi or bacteria
   c. potatoes and squash
   d. new species of cotton, corn, soybeans, and sugar beets

____ 5. Which of the following conclusions can the reader infer from the passage?
   a. Bioengineering is illegal.
   b. Bioengineering is thought to be dangerous by most scientists.
   c. Bioengineering is used by farmers everywhere.
   d. Biotechnology has critics around the world.

B. Directions: Decide if the following statements are valid inferences that are firmly based on the information in the above passage.

____ 6. Farming has become extremely dangerous.
   a. valid inference
   b. not a valid inference

____ 7. Most people aren't affected by genetic engineering in agriculture.
   a. valid inference
   b. not a valid inference

____ 8. Agricultural biotechnology is used to grow crops that will prevent common diseases in humans.
   a. valid inference
   b. not a valid inference

____ 9. The safety of agricultural biotechnology is questionable.
   a. valid inference
   b. not a valid inference

___ 10. Farmers can save money and time by growing bio-engineered crops.
   a. valid inference
   b. not a valid inference

Chapter 12: The Basics of Argument
LAB 12.1 PRACTICE EXERCISE 1

Name_____ Section _____ Date _____ Score (number correct) _____ x 10 = _____

Objective: To identify the claim and support in an argument.

A. Directions: Read all of the statements for each question and choose the claim.

_____1. Which one of the following sentences states the claim for this group of ideas (taken from the text *Business Ethics: A Managerial Approach* by Wicks, et. al., p. 221)?
  a. Wal-Mart expanded its services, including groceries, florists, pharmacies, and optical.
  b. Wal-Mart's presence has driven small local stores, such as the "Mom and Pop" stores as well as many large retailers, out of town or out of business.
  c. When Wal-Mart moved into the supermarket business in Las Vegas, 18 of the California-based Raley's Supermarkets closed, laying off 14,000 workers.
  d. The 920 Southeast grocery chain Winn-Dixie's bankruptcy in 2004 was in part attributed to Wal-Mart.

_____2. Which one of the following sentences states the claim for this group of ideas (taken from the text by Elizabeth Goldsmith, *Consumer Economics: Issues and Behaviors*, 2nd ed., p. 106)?
  a. Johnson & Johnson cultivates a powerful image as "the caring company," associated with products for cuddly babies.
  b. United Parcel Service, Microsoft, and Toyota score high in exemplary service surveys.
  c. When Hope Dept dropped to nineteenth place in 2001 from fourth in 2000, it made some changes, such as having salespeople unpack merchandise at night so they could help customers during prime shopping hours.
  d. Customer service is a critical part of the consumer experience, which plays into customer satisfaction and expectations.

_____3. Which one of the following sentences states the claim for this group of ideas (adapted from the text written by Ciccarelli and White, *Psychology*, 2nd ed., p. 442)?
  a. Avoidance-avoidance conflicts are very stressful and people will often go to great lengths to avoid them.
  b. Avoidance-avoidance conflicts are often symbolized by common phrases, such as "caught between a rock and a hard place."
  c. Given the choice of risky back surgery or living with the pain, many people will wait, hoping that the pain will go away on its own.
  d. People who are fearful of dental procedures might chose to suffer the pain of a toothache instead of going to the dentist.

B. Directions: Read the paragraph and determine whether the sentences state the claim or support for an argument.

[1]Parents can be effective in reducing the negative effects of viewing television in general and violent television in particular. [2]Parents should watch television with their child; not only does watching television with children provide parents with information about what children are seeing, but active discussion and explanation of television programs can increase children's comprehension of content, reduce stereotypical thinking, and increase pro-social behavior.

_____ 4. Sentence 1 states the _____.
    a. claim
    b. support
    c. This sentence is not relevant information.

_____ 5. Sentence 2 states the _____.
    a. claim
    b. support
    c. This sentence is not relevant information

C. Directions: Select the statement that is *not* relevant to the claim presented.

_____ 6. Claim: One reason our state revenue is down is that the past legislature abolished parole.
    a. The prison population has increased: by 2009, even if prisoners double-bunk, state prisons will still need 11,000 additional cells.
    b. In previous years, the state rented out unused cells to alleviate overcrowding in other states.
    c. Our state has lost $70 million as a result of the decision to abolish parole.
    d. This year three prisoners were exonerated as a result of new DNA testing.

_____ 7. Claim: Voters should be willing to raise taxes in order to address some critical mental health needs.
    a. "On a good day, our state ranks 47th in mental health," stated Delegate Phil Hamilton at a recent town meeting.
    b. In the 21-or-older age bracket, the waiting list for a group home consists of 2,000 people.
    c. Virginia does not impose a one-cent tax on imported tobacco products.
    d. Recently, one desperate elderly woman who is the sole caregiver for her critically ill husband sought the help of Delegate Glenn Oder and was able to get her mentally challenged son bumped up to the short waiting list for a group home; however, this list is currently six years long.

_____ 8. Claim: The reality shows on television are more contrived voyeurism than entertainment.
    a. Many of the people selected for the shows are beautiful and handsome, not at all like real people.
    b. The shows are scripted, although they are presented as an unfolding of actual events.
    c. One of the first reality shows, Survivor, created a national folk hero with Rudy, the former Navy seal.
    d. Each episode feeds the audiences' needs for more sensationalism, profanity, and vulgar behavior, which require the scrutiny of censors.

_____ 9. Claim: Television is diminishing our attention span.
    a. A flash of light signals our brains to flee, freeze, or fight and since we are in a safe environment, our bodies remain stationary, which prompts the behavior of a couch potato.
    b. Most segments of television shows are 12 to 14 minutes with commercial interruptions, and that is about the same length of time students can pay attention during a lecture.
    c. According to pediatricians, babies under the age of two should not be allowed to watch television.
    d. Babies should not be left in a child carrier for long periods of time since that position will not help develop their peripheral vision.

164

___ 10. U.S. children are not getting enough sleep and the consequences are taking a toll on the quality of their lives.
   a. Just before going to bed, children are in the habit of watching television in their rooms, which can be too stimulating.
   b. One study recently showed that sleep-deprivation in truck drivers mimicked the same symptoms of being legally drunk.
   c. Many children have one or more beverages with caffeine before going to bed, which inhibits their ability to fall asleep.
   d. Sleep deprivation has been attributed to learning problems and obesity in children.

Name _____ Section _____ Date _____ Score (number correct) _____ x 10 = _____

Objective: To identify the claim and support in an argument.

A. Directions: Read all of the statements for each question and choose the claim.

____ 1. Which one of the following sentences states the claim for this group of ideas?
   a. States should adopt a plan for chartered universities and colleges.
   b. The school officials would agree to maintain the ratio of in-state to out-of-state students, giving preference to state residents.
   c. Given more independence in areas such as tuition increases, the colleges would then ask for less money from the state.
   d. Currently, universities and colleges are losing talented professors to states that offer more lucrative jobs.

____ 2. Which one of the following sentences states the claim for this group of ideas?
   a. Over 12 million pets end up in shelters each year.
   b. The majority of pets in shelters end up being put to sleep.
   c. Purchasing a pet can cost up to $5,000, but adopting a pet may cost only between $10 and $300.
   d. Adopting a rescued pet can fill a need for both the owner and the animal, and it is a practical way of acquiring a new family friend.

B. Directions: Read the following outline of a point and its supports. Decide if each support is relevant to the claim or if it is not relevant to the claim.

Claim: Music is an important aspect of our lives and should be taught to all students at all levels.

Support:

____ 3. The heavy bass of some popular music has been shown to increase blood pressure, which can increase anger in older adults.
   a. relevant
   b. not relevant

Support:

____ 4. Listening to Mozart promotes students' ability to complete complex math problems.
   a. relevant
   b. not relevant

Support:

____ 5. Students who learn to play musical instruments tend to perform well in math classes because they have been schooled in sequencing.
   a. relevant
   b. not relevant

Support:

____ 6. Music can also help students in anger management since playing an instrument offers an outlet for frustrations, and listening to some genres, such as "New Age," lowers blood pressure.
a. relevant
b. not relevant

Claim: To be a savvy consumer, shoppers need to be vigilant and coached in how to scrutinize sales promotions.

Support:

____ 7. Some companies now have a "restocking fee," which is to be paid by the customer who wants to return an item.
a. relevant
b. not relevant

Support:

____ 8. Linens and furniture buys often appear in January and February.
a. relevant
b. not relevant

Support:

____ 9. Car sales in states with a personal property tax tend to be lower at the end of the year, so a consumer may find the best buy if he or she patiently waits until December.
a. relevant
b. not relevant

Support:

___ 10. While they have become very popular, SUVs are a hazard to other drivers.
a. relevant
b. not relevant

Chapter 12: The Basics of Argument
LAB 12.3 REVIEW TEST 1

Name _____ Section _____ Date _____ Score (number correct) _____ x 10 = _____

A. Directions: Read all of the statements for each question and choose the claim.

_____ 1. Which one of the following sentences states the claim for this group of ideas?
  a. Over 12 million pets end up in shelters each year.
  b. The majority of pets in shelters end up being put to sleep.
  c. Purchasing a pet can cost up to $5,000, but adopting a pet may cost only between $10 and $300.
  d. Adopting a rescued pet can fill a need for both the owner and the family.

_____ 2. Which one of the following sentences states the claim for this group of ideas?
  a. Nonmedical use of narcotic pain relievers, tranquilizers, stimulants, and sedatives ranks second (behind marijuana) as a category of illicit drug abuse among adults and youth.
  b. In 2002, 6.2 million Americans were current abusers of prescription drugs.
  c. Recent data indicate that prescription drug abuse, particularly of opioid pain killers, has increased at an alarming rate over the last ten years.
  d. Emergency-room visits resulting from narcotic pain-reliever abuse have increased 163 percent since 1998.

_____ 3. Which one of the following sentences states the claim for this group of ideas?
  a. Fuel load consists of dead and dying trees, dense undergrowth, and stands of small trees.
  b. Effective forest management must include fuel reduction through logging and controlled burning.
  c. The acreage of dead and dying wood and vegetation is increasing in scope and density because of tree diseases caused by fungi and insect infestation.
  d. Fuel load is a major culprit for the recent increase in wildfires.

B. Directions: Read the following outline of a point and its supports. Decide if each support is relevant to the claim or if it is not relevant to the claim.

Claim: Many first-year college students need to be apprised of the ethics of academia.

Supports

_____ 4. Recently, a student was suspended when he lied to his history professor about the reason he was not able to take the scheduled midterm.
  a. relevant
  b. not relevant

_____ 5. One student researched the engineering marvel of the pyramids of Egypt.
  a. relevant
  b. not relevant

_____ 6. When confronted for plagiarism by her English teacher, one coed recently replied, "What do you mean, I was cheating? I paid good money for that paper."
   a. relevant
   b. not relevant

_____ 7. An engineering instructor at another institution "googled" her students' research papers and discovered that 8 out of 15 students did not cite their sources.
   a. relevant
   b. not relevant

C. Directions: Read the following passage and answer the questions that follow.

Overload

[1]Have you ever felt that the pressures of life were building up so that you could no longer meet their demands? [2]Perhaps you felt as though there simply wasn't enough time in the day for you to accomplish all the things you needed to do. [3]During this time you may have noticed a decline in your social life and more of a "self-centeredness." [4]Perhaps you lost sleep and so became tired and irritable. [5]You may even have become more susceptible to colds and flu. [6]If any of these things sounds familiar, chances are you were a victim of overload. [7]*Overload*, which means the same as overstimulation, refers to the state in which the demands around you exceed your capacity to meet them. [8]Some aspects of your life are placing excessive demands on you. [9]When these demands exceed your ability to comply with them, you experience distress. [10]*Overload*: a level of stimulation or demand that exceeds the capacity to process or comply with that input; overstimulation.

[11]The four major factors in overload are (1) time pressures, (2) excessive responsibilities, (3) lack of support, and (4) excessive expectations from yourself and those around you. [12]Any one or a combination of these factors can result in stress from overload. [13]Overload encompasses the city, the occupational environment, the school, and even the home. [14]Interestingly, many people are able to accomplish significantly high levels of success with no sign of overload distress.

—Adapted from Girdano, Everly, and Dusek, *Controlling Stress and Tension*, 6th ed., p. 126.

_____ 8. Which claim is adequately supported by the evidence in the passage?
   a. The single most significant cause of overload arises from the excessive demands of others.
   b. Overload can be avoided by learning to say no to others.
   c. Overload is a significant and pervasive stressor in modern society.
   d. Overload leads to serious mental and physical health risks.

_____ 9. In the first paragraph, sentence 4 states _____.
   a. a detail that is relevant
   b. a detail that is not relevant

___ 10. In the second paragraph, sentence 14 states _____.
   a. a detail that is relevant
   b. a detail that is not relevant

169

Chapter 12: The Basics of Argument
LAB 12.4 REVIEW TEST 2

Name_____ Section _____ Date _____ Score (number correct) _____ x 10 = _____

A. **Directions**: Read all of the statements for each question and choose the claim.

_____ 1. Which one of the following sentences states the claim for this group of ideas (adapted from Joseph DeVito, in the text *The Interpersonal Communication Book*, 12th ed., pp. 155–156)?
a. In China, red signifies prosperity and rebirth and is used for festive and joyous occasions.
b. In France and the United Kingdom, red indicates masculinity.
c. In many African countries red indicates blasphemy or death.
d. Colors vary greatly in their meanings from one culture to another.

_____ 2. Which one of the following sentences states the claim for this group of ideas (adapted from the text by Dale, et. al., *Human Behavior and the Social Environment: Social Systems Theory*, 6th ed., p. 232)?
a. Marriage is no longer a requisite for socially sanctioned childbearing.
b. For a whole economic class of people, the single-parent (which means *single-mother* in most cases) family is normative.
c. The traditional concept of family is outmoded.
d. Same-sex couples may now seek social sanction to raise children.

_____ 3. Which one of the following sentences states the claim for this group of ideas (adapted from the text written by Macionis, *Sociology*, 13th ed., p. 403)?
a. Oregon physicians can legally assist in ending the lives of patients.
b. A person facing extreme suffering should be able to choose to live or die.
c. Netherlands has the most permissive euthanasia law in the world.
d. Surveys show that two-thirds of U.S. adults support giving people the option of dying with a doctor's help.

B. Directions: Read the following outline of a point and its supports. Decide if each support is relevant to the claim or if it is not relevant to the claim.

Claim: Television is diminishing our attention span.

Supports:

_____ 4. A flash of light signals our brains to flee, freeze, or fight and since we are in a safe environment, our bodies remain stationary, which prompts the behavior of a couch potato.
a. relevant
b. not relevant

_____ 5. Most segments of television shows are 12 to 14 minutes with commercial interruptions, and that is about the same length of time students can pay attention during a lecture.
a. relevant
b. not relevant

____ 6. According to pediatricians, babies under the age of two should not be allowed to watch television.
   a. relevant
   b. not relevant

____ 7. Babies should not be left in a child carrier for long periods of time since that position hinders the development of their peripheral vision.
   a. relevant
   b. not relevant

C. Directions: Read the passage and answer the questions that follow.

[1]Easy access to firearms in the United States leads to more violence than any other nation. In 1992, 367 people were killed by handguns in Great Britain, Sweden, Switzerland, Japan, Australia, and Canada combined. [2]The total population of those countries equaled that of the United States, where in that same year, handguns killed 13,200 people. [3]Public opinion polls showed that most Americans favored gun control. [4]The powerful gun lobby and the National Rifle Association, however, argued that the Second Amendment to the Constitution guaranteed individuals the unlimited right to bear arms. [5]Access to firearms remained easy.

—Adapted from Jones et al., Created Equal: *A History of the United States*, Combined Volume, brief 3rd ed., p. 671.

____ 8. Sentence 1 is a statement that is _____.
   a. a claim
   b. support for a claim

____ 9. Sentence 2 is a statement that is _____.
   a. a claim
   b. support for a claim

____ 10. Sentence 4 is a statement that is _____.
   a. a claim
   b. support for a claim

Name_____ Section _____ Date _____ Score (number correct) _____ x 10 = _____

A. Directions: Read all of the statements for each question and choose the claim.

_____ 1. Which one of the following sentences states the claim for this group of ideas?
    a. The male has a pouch he may inflate with water to attract females, who may compete to win him.
    b. The term pregnancy is appropriate, for the male's pouch functions as more than a depository; it provides nourishing oxygen and fluids through a capillary network.
    c. During mating, the female impregnates the male, depositing 200-600 pinkish eggs from .5 to 1.5 mm in diameter into the male pouch.
    d. The reproductive service provided by male seahorses is unique in the animal kingdom.

_____ 2. Which one of the following sentences states the claim for this group of ideas?
    a. Consuming a moderate amount of alcohol can reduce stress and anxiety while improving self-confidence.
    b. Intake of a moderate amount of alcohol can improve appetite and dietary intake in the elderly.
    c. Moderate alcohol consumption has been linked to lower rates of heart disease.
    d. In most people, moderate alcohol intake offers some psychological benefits.

B. Directions: Read the following outline of a point and its supports. Decide if each support is relevant to the claim or if it is not relevant to the claim.

Claim: Low-carbohydrate diets are not a safe long-term solution for weight loss.

Support:

_____ 3. Low-carbohydrate diets are high in fat which contribute to heart disease.
    a. relevant
    b. not relevant

Support:

_____ 4. Low-carbohydrate diets can be deficient in several nutrients.
    a. relevant
    b. not relevant

Support:

_____ 5. Any diet that prohibits certain types or categories of food is very difficult to maintain long-term.
    a. relevant
    b. not relevant

Support:

_____ 6. Most diets usually do not focus on portion control, which can be a major factor in weight loss.
a. relevant
b. not relevant

C. Directions: Read the following passage and answer the questions that follow.

[1]Latin America has severe financial problems. [2]Latin America has the most uneven distribution of wealth in the world, and the gap between rich and poor has increased in recent decades. [3]The largely failed efforts at economic liberalization during the 1980s and 1990s have only exacerbated matters further, as the real value of workers' wages has continued to decline over this period. [4]150 million Latin Americans still live on less than $2 a day. [5]Educational, health, and sanitation services are inadequate, and literacy rates remain low. [6]Health issues are a major concern also. [7]Life expectancy for Latin American males is around 55 years—17 years less than in the United States and Canada. [8]Consequently, Latin America has severe problems and needs intervention if the country is to thrive.

—Adapted from Edgar, Hackett, Jewsbury, Molony, and Gordon, *Civilizations Past & Present, Vol. II, From 1300*, 12th ed., 1032.

_____ 7. Sentence 1 is a statement that is _____.
a. a claim
b. support for a claim

_____ 8. Sentence 4 is a statement that is _____.
a. a claim
b. support for a claim

_____ 9. Sentence 6 is a statement that is _____.
a. a claim
b. support for a claim

_____ 10. Sentence 8 is a statement that is _____.
a. a claim
b. support for a claim

Name_____ Section _____ Date _____ Score (number correct) _____ x 10 = _____

A. Directions: Read all of the statements for each question and choose the claim.

_____ 1. Which one of the following sentences states the claim for this group of ideas?
   a. As the pressure to be thin mounts, some female athletes begin to engage in disordered eating behaviors.
   b. Thinness in females may disrupt the menstrual cycle and result in amenorrhea.
   c. Sports that emphasize leanness increase the risk of serious medical disorders in women athletes.
   d. Osteoporosis can result without the normal reproductive hormones.

_____ 2.   Which one of the following sentences states the claim for this group of ideas?
   a. Children and adolescents who are overweight are at greater risk for type 2 diabetes, elevated blood pressure, and other medical problems.
   b. Managing the weight of children is a serious concern for the United States.
   c. Children in the United States are experiencing the same trends of inappropriate weight gain seen in the adult population.
   d. More than 17% of children age 6 to 19 are overweight.

_____ 3. Which one of the following sentences states the claim for this group of ideas adapted from the college text—DeVito, *Messages: Building Interpersonal Communication Skills,* 4th ed., p. 331.
   a. The fluoride in our water is damaging our children's health.
   b. Consuming too much fluoride causes the teeth to become stained and pitted.
   c. Teeth seem to be at the highest risk for fluorosis during the first eight years of life.
   d. Excess fluoride can cause fluorosis of our skeleton.

B. Directions: Read the following outline of a point and its supports. Decide if each support is relevant to the claim or if it is not relevant to the claim.

Claim: It is in the best interest of the federal government to raise appropriate funding for the treatment of patients with Alzheimer's disease.

Support:

_____ 4. The current economic impact of Alzheimer's on America is $100 billion a year for care (medical and custodial) and another $33 billion in work hours lost by caregivers.
   a. relevant
   b. not relevant

Support:

_____5. It is extremely important for the Alzheimer's patient to have designated a trusted surrogate to make end-of-life decisions.
   a. relevant
   b. not relevant

Support:

_____ 6. Unless a preventive vaccine, a cure, or better treatment drugs are found, 14 million Americans will be ill with the disease in 2050.
    a. relevant
    b. not relevant

B. Directions: Read the paragraph and answer the questions that follow.

[1]In modern commercial agriculture, nutrients are added artificially to the soil. [2]These nutrients may be delivered in the form of animal manure, by plowing into the soil a soil-enriching crop, or as manufactured inorganic fertilizers. [3]The more intensively a soil is worked, the more important such additions become. [4]Unfortunately, this agriculture activity is proving to be a serious concern for our country. [5]Increasing these artificial nutrients means that organic matter is not being replaced as rapidly as it is withdrawn. [6]Soil fertility usually declines over decades, so the problem is less apparent than if it occurred over just a few years. [7]Variations in crop yield from year to year are caused by weather, insects, plant diseases, and changing technology.

—Adapted from Bergman and Renwick, *Introduction to Geography: People, Places, and Environment*, 4th ed., p. 147–148.

_____ 7. Which one of the following sentences states the claim for this paragraph?
    a. sentence 1
    b. sentence 2
    c. sentence 3
    d. sentence 4

_____ 8. Sentence 2 is a statement that is _____.
    a. a claim
    b. support for a claim

_____ 9. Sentence 5 is a statement that is _____.
    a. a claim
    b. support for a claim

_____ 10. Which sentence is NOT a valid support for the claim?
    a. sentence 4
    b. sentence 5
    c. sentence 6
    d. sentence 7

Name_____ Section _____ Date _____ Score (number correct) _____ x 10 = _____

Objective: To identify fallacies of logic and propaganda techniques.

Directions: Choose the fallacy used in each of the following items.

_____ 1. Everyone should eat a nutritious bowl of oatmeal on a daily basis for its health benefits.
    a. either-or
    b. begging the question
    c. straw man
    d. false cause

_____ 2. By teaching sexual education in public schools, educators are exposing children to the dangerous temptations of pre-marital sex.
    a. either-or
    b. false comparison
    c. false cause
    d. begging the question

_____ 3. Governor Schwazen's deep alliance with the liberal Hollywood crowd and the extreme social activists of groups like PETA and Greenpeace becomes more apparent each day he is in office.
    a. personal attack
    b. false cause
    c. begging the question
    d. false comparison

_____ 4. The college once again raised tuition because the administration is more concerned about making a profit than they are about educating students.
    a. begging the question
    b. either-or
    c. false cause
    d. straw man

_____ 5. Either reduce serving sizes in restaurants or stop complaining about people who are obese.
    a. either-or
    b. begging the question
    c. false cause
    d. straw man

B. Directions: Identify the propaganda technique used in each of the following items.

_____ 6. All politicians are crooks. They have to be corrupt to survive as a politician.
    a. plain folks
    b. name calling
    c. transfer
    d. bandwagon

_____ 7. In order to ensure a prosperous future for our children, we must raise the retirement age to 70. By taking this brave and selfless step, we save the most successful program in the history of a democracy—Social Security.
   a. bandwagon
   b. transfer
   c. testimonial
   d. glittering generalities

_____ 8. Candidate Plecher stands with George Washington, Abraham Lincoln, and Harry Truman in his commitment to the preservation of the United States
   a. transfer
   b. glittering generalities
   c. bandwagon
   d. plain folks

_____ 9. Candidate Plecher has proven his courage as a solider on the battlefield, his integrity as a businessman in the board room, and his compassion as an educator in the school room.
   a. plain folks
   b. false cause
   c. testimonial
   d. glittering generalities

_____ 10. Although elected into office as a Republican, Senator Jamal announced three weeks ago that he will be changing his party affiliation to the Democratic party because he is outraged by the Republican economic platform. However, investigative reporters learned that shortly before Jamal made his announcement, he was offered a key leadership position in the Democratic party.
   a. card stacking
   b. bandwagon
   c. transfer
   d. plain folks

Name_____ Section _____ Date _____ Score (number correct) _____ x 10 = _____

Objective: To identify fallacies of logic and propaganda techniques.

Directions: Choose the fallacy used in each of the following items.

_____ 1. Pete Rose should never be allowed into Baseball's Hall of Fame because he is an unethical cheat who sold out his team for personal profit.
   a. begging the question
   b. personal attack
   c. straw man
   d. either-or

_____ 2. Either limit the numbers of students in each classroom or accept lower student achievement.
   a. either-or
   b. personal attack
   c. straw man
   d. false cause

_____ 3. Evolution is not true because life did not evolve over millions of years.
   a. begging the question
   b. personal attack
   c. straw man
   d. false comparison

_____ 4. In 1868, the leaders of the Democratic Party were Horatio Seymour, known as the Rioter; Nathan Bedford Forrest, the Butcher; Raphael Semmes, the Pirate; and Wade Hampton, the Hangman.
   a. either-or
   b. begging the question
   b. personal attack
   c. straw man

_____ 5. Laws that require motorcyclists to wear helmets infringe on a person's freedom of the pursuit of happiness.
   a. begging the question
   b. personal attack
   c. straw man
   d. false comparison

B. Directions: Identify the propaganda technique used in each of the following items.

_____ 6. Just like my parents and my entire family, I stand against cloning
   a. name-calling
   b. testimonial
   c. band wagon
   d. transfer

_____ 7. A vote for Julio Rodriquez is a vote for equality, peace, and prosperity.
   a. glittering generalities
   b. testimonial
   c. card stacking
   d. band wagon

_____ 8. A radio commercial states, "All you hard-working families, listen up! Speedy Lube will change your oil in 10 minutes for $10. You can't get a better deal than that! Hurry on in."
   a. plain folks
   b. name-calling
   c. glittering generalities
   d. transfer

_____ 9. Film critic Roger Ebert proclaimed, "The *Star Wars* Film saga, like all great literature, tells a timeless story of man's universal and individual struggle with good and evil."
   a. testimonial
   b. glittering generalities
   c. plain folks
   d. transfer

___ 10. A scholarly-looking man dressed in a conservative suit sits on the edge of an executive desk in a private office and says, "Studies prove that Relorax helps manage stress."
   a. name-calling
   b. plain folks
   c. transfer
   d. testimonial

Name_____ Section _____ Date _____ Score (number correct) _____ x 10 = _____

A. Directions: Identify the fallacy used in each of the following items.

_____ 1. We must pay higher taxes or cut social programs.
   a. begging the question
   b. personal attack
   c. either-or
   d. false comparison

_____ 2. Laws that require motorcyclists to wear helmets infringe on a person's freedom of the pursuit of happiness.
   a. begging the question
   b. personal attack
   c. straw man
   d. either-or

_____ 3. Ms. Bailey seeks the office of Mayor of Phoenix as the first step in her bid for a political career in the national arena. She cares about the people of Phoenix as future voters who can catapult her into greater power. She cares nothing about the needs of the community.
   a. begging the question
   b. personal attack
   c. straw man
   d. false comparison

_____ 4. Those who support euthanasia have no respect for the sanctity of life.
   a. false cause
   b. personal attack
   c. begging the question
   d. straw man

_____ 5. The movie *Million Dollar Baby* begins as a feel-good story about a young woman boxer overcoming all odds. Suddenly, the plot twists when the woman sustains a debilitating injury and asks her boxing coach to help her end her life. Critics claim that the movie's director, Clint Eastwood, is propagating support for euthanasia and undermining the value of life as a disabled person.
   a. straw man
   b. begging the question
   c. either-or
   d. false comparison

180

B. Directions: Identify the propaganda technique used in each of the following items.

____ 6. I dropped Professor Patel's class because he is a radical who preaches instead of teaches.
   a. plain folks
   b. bandwagon
   c. testimonial
   d. name-calling

____ 7. If you want to help others, if you want to make a difference with your life, if you want to see results, if you want to work hard, if you want to work with others who share these same values, join Home For You, and help us build homes for the homeless.
   a. plain folks
   b. glittering generalities
   c. bandwagon
   d. name-calling

____ 8. The public either believes talk show hosts or it believes the truth.
   a. plain folks.
   b. bandwagon.
   c. testimonial
   d. either-or

____ 9. Rush Limbaugh answered Tom Daschle's criticism by pointing out to his listeners that every time liberal politicians lose, they blame talk radio or they blame the people.
   a. plain folks
   b. false cause
   c. testimonial
   d. name-calling

___ 10. A national restaurant chain runs the following advertising campaign: "Are you hungry for a home-cooked, nutritious meal? Are you searching for a relaxing and pleasant place to gather with friends and family? Come to our house, and let our family serve your family."
   a. plain folks
   b. false comparison
   c. testimonial
   d. name-calling

Name_____ Section _____ Date _____ Score (number correct) _____ x 10 = _____

A. Directions: Identify the fallacy used in each of the follow items.

_____ 1. Reality shows are extremely popular because they make so much money from the huge audiences that watch them.
   a. either-or
   b. false comparison
   c. false cause
   d. begging the question

_____ 2. Forcing children to attend church is like herding cattle to slaughter. The children are driven into the pews by their parents where they are systematically 'put to sleep' by the service.
   a. either-or
   b. false comparison
   c. false cause
   d. begging the question

_____ 3. If you purchase an SUV, you don't care about the environment. Everyone knows that an SUV ruins the environment, guzzles gas, and is a foolish waste of money.
   a. either-or
   b. false comparison
   c. false cause
   d. begging the question

_____ 4. The company agreed to pay the back wages of the employees who had been fired six months ago only if the employees agreed to sign a document stating that they were guilty of maligning the reputation of the company and deserved to be fired.
   a. either-or
   b. false comparison
   c. false cause
   d. begging the question

_____ 5. Everyone knows the mayor shouldn't have been elected because he didn't even graduate from high school, and he never even served in the military. How could such a man be a credit to the town? There is no way people should put their trust in him.
   a. straw man
   b. false comparison
   c. false cause
   d. personal attack

B. Directions: Identify the propaganda technique used in each of the following items.

_____ 6. If Oprah Winfrey supports an author on her show, the author's book often becomes an instant best seller.
   a.   bandwagon
   b.   transfer
   c.   plain folks
   d.   glittering generalities

_____ 7. You parents have been contacted about these dire events, because if we don't raise enough money to buy instruments for the school symphony, the love for fine arts will disappear in our schools and our children will never nurture a love for classical music that is so important for our cultural heritage.
   a.   bandwagon
   b.   transfer
   c.   plain folks
   d.   glittering generalities

_____ 8. All veterans have joined the fight against allowing illegal aliens to become citizens of the United States, so you should do the same. Write your local congressmen and support your veterans by joining this cause.
   a.   bandwagon
   b.   transfer
   c.   plain folks
   d.   glittering generalities

_____ 9. Come and join Senator Robb and the rest of the townsfolk in a down-home country barbecue, and enjoy the music of the local blue-grass band as we celebrate a good-old fashioned 4th of July.
   a.   bandwagon
   b.   transfer
   c.   plain folks
   d.   glittering generalities

C. Directions: Read the following fictitious advertisement. Identify the detail that would be omitted from the advertisement by card stacking.

___ 10. Want to get rid of those unsightly wrinkles and look years younger? Botox does help, but with the amazing Product X, you can avoid needles and injections.
   a.   Product X is a cream prepared from natural extracts.
   b.   You can get your free trial of Product X online.
   c.   You may have to pay up to $12.00 in mailing expenses and your credit card will be charged $69.00 for Product X if you decide to keep it.
   d.   Product X is the best one in the market to treat the fine lines, dark under eye circles and wrinkles on the forehead.

Name _____ Section _____ Date _____ Score (number correct) _____ x 10 = _____

A. Directions: Identify the fallacy used in each of the following items.

_____ 1. Politicians and judges who support euthanasia have no regard for human life.
    a. false cause
    b. begging the question
    c. either-or
    d. straw man

_____ 2. Professor Meecham should be removed from his position at the university. He spends more time writing and publishing his ideas than he spends teaching his students.
    a. false comparison
    b. straw man
    c. false cause
    d. either-or

_____ 3. Beware of the organization PeaceForAllLife.com; this group is made up of radical environmentalists who believe that the rodent's life and habitat are more important than the farmer's right to farm the land.
    a. straw man
    b. false cause
    c. begging the question
    d. personal attack

_____ 4. Tom Daschle also said that radio-talk show hosts, like religious fundamentalists in other countries, stir their followers into emotional frenzies: "You know, we see it in foreign countries and we think, 'Well, my God, how can this religious fundamentalism become so violent?' Well, it's that same shrill rhetoric, it's that same shrill power that motivates. Somebody says something and then it becomes a little more shrill the next time. And then more shrill the next time. And pretty soon it's a foment that becomes physical in addition to just verbal."
    a. straw man
    b. false cause
    c. false comparison
    d. either-or

_____ 5. George W. Bush, the 43rd President of the United States, ordered the invasion of Iraq in 2003 to complete his father's goal in the Gulf War of removing Saddam Hussein from power.
    a. false comparison
    b. straw man
    c. false cause
    d. either-or

B. Directions: Identify the propaganda technique used in each of the following items.

_____ 6. In a 1998 article published in the *LA Weekly*, Harold Meyerson called Republican Assemblywoman Barbara Alby "a primitive out of the GOP's Taliban wing."
   a. false comparison
   b. glittering generalities
   c. name calling
   d. plain folks

_____ 7. A candidate for the senate appears at a local rally wearing the cap of the area's professional baseball team, a plaid long–sleeved shirt with the sleeves rolled up, and jeans. His wife and teenage son and daughter appear with him. In his speech, he says, "Susan and I are honored to have your support. Like you, we want to take our country away from the professional politicians and place the power back in the hands of the people who make this country great."
   a. transfer
   b. testimonial
   c. bandwagon
   d. plain folks

_____ 8. A politician who has consistently voted against raising taxes votes with the majority in his party to institute a federal sales tax on goods and services. When questioned by the media, she states, "The polls clearly indicate that people don't want any cuts in government services, and my party is convinced that the federal sales tax is the correct solution, so I vote with the people and with my party."
   a. testimonial
   b. transfer
   c. glittering generalities
   d. bandwagon

_____ 9. A famous actor appears as himself in a commercial for Eight O'clock coffee stating, "I love the rich aroma, the warm and satisfying taste of Eight O'clock any time of the day!"
   a. testimonial
   b. transfer
   c. glittering generalities
   d. bandwagon

C. Directions: Read the following fictitious advertisement. Identify the detail that was **omitted** from the advertisement for the purpose of card stacking.

_____ 10. This three-bedroom, two-bath town house is priced to sell at $172,000. Recently renovated, this 1500-square-foot home is in ready-to-move-in condition. Small private back yard is beautifully landscaped with a deck that overlooks a natural preserve. Large eat-in kitchen, fireplace, and a whirlpool tub in the master bathroom.
   a. The house is priced under its appraised price.
   b. The owners need to sell quickly.
   c. The house shows signs of termite damage.
   d. The seller will help pay closing costs.

Name_____ Section _____ Date _____ Score (number correct) _____ x 10 = _____

A. Directions: Identify the fallacy used in each of the following items.

_____ 1. Either we cut the social programs or we live with a huge federal deficit, and we cannot afford a huge federal deficit.
  a. either-or
  b. straw man
  c. false cause
  d. false comparison

_____ 2. In 2005, Moveon.org created an advertisement to run in the *New York Times* that stated, "First George Bush said Saddam Hussein had weapons of mass destruction and a 'mushroom cloud' was imminent. Now, he's claiming something equally outrageous: a phony social-security crisis."
  a. begging the question
  b. false cause
  c. false comparison
  d. straw man

_____ 3. In a 2002 column that appeared in National Review Online, Ron Unz, then chairman of English for the Children, stated, "While most Americans have been transfixed by the terrifying prospect of massive deaths from anthrax or suicide bombers, a few in our society fear an even greater horror: The fanatic defenders of Spanish-almost-always instruction see their doom in an 'English' initiative heading toward the November 2002 Massachusetts ballot."
  a. personal attack
  b. false cause
  c. either-or
  d. begging the question

_____ 4. Obese people should lose weight because they are overweight.
  a. begging the question
  b. false cause
  c. either-or
  d. false comparison

_____ 5. I took the natural supplement Echinacea, and my cold went away.
  a. false comparison
  b. false cause
  c. personal attack
  d. straw man

B. Directions: Identify the propaganda technique used in each of the following items.

____ 6. To draw attention to the needs of boys who may be at risk, Laura Bush attends a Passport to Manhood program and listens to young boys share ideas about respect and love during a visit to the Germantown Boys and Girls Club, Tuesday, Feb. 3, 2005, in Philadelphia.
   a. bandwagon
   b. transfer
   c. plain folks
   d. glittering generalities

____ 7. This charming ranch house sits on a wooded lot overlooking a natural preserve.
   a. card stacking
   b. name calling
   c. plain folks
   d. glittering generalities

____ 8. In his weekly radio address on February 26, 2005, President Bush said, "Saving Social Security will not be easy, but if you make clear that you expect your leaders to confront problems head on, not pass them on to future generations, I am confident that we will put aside partisan politics in Washington and meet our duty to you, the American people."
   a. name calling
   b. testimonial
   c. plain folks
   d. glittering generalities

____ 9. Every radical in Congress voted for Women's Suffrage.
   a. transfer
   b. bandwagon
   c. name calling
   d. plain folks

C. Directions: Read the following fictitious advertisement. Identify the detail that was **omitted** from the advertisement for the purpose of card stacking.

____ 10. This 2002 Dodge pickup is in immaculate condition: pristine white, plush seats and floor mats, low mileage, well-maintained. Priced to sell. Call soon.
   a. The pickup has an extended warranty.
   b. The pickup gets 20 miles to the gallon in gas mileage.
   c. The pickup has new tires.
   d. The pickup has been subject to several major recalls from the factory.

Name_____ Date _____

Objective: To practice for the *Florida College Basic Skills Exit Reading Test*.

Use this answer sheet for the practice test, *Florida College Basic Skills Exit Reading Test,* in your textbook. Fill in the correct answer for each numbered item. Be sure to choose only one answer for each numbered item.

_____1._____ 15. _____ 29.

_____2._____ 16. _____ 30.

_____3._____ 17. _____ 31.

_____4._____ 18. _____ 32.

_____5._____ 19. _____ 33.

_____6._____ 20. _____ 34.

_____7._____ 21. _____ 35.

_____8._____ 22. _____ 36.

_____9._____ 23. _____ 37.

_____10._____ 24. _____ 38.

_____11._____ 25. _____ 39.

_____12._____ 26. _____ 40.

_____13._____ 27.

_____14._____ 28.

Name_____ Date _____

Objective: To gain more practice for the *Florida College Basic Skills Exit Reading Test.*

Fill in the correct answer for each numbered item. Be sure to choose only one answer for each numbered item.

_____ 1._____ 15. _____ 29.

_____ 2._____ 16. _____ 30.

_____ 3._____ 17. _____ 31.

_____ 4._____ 18. _____ 32.

_____ 5._____ 19. _____ 33.

_____ 6._____ 20. _____ 34.

_____ 7._____ 21. _____ 35.

_____ 8._____ 22. _____ 36.

_____ 9._____ 23. _____ 37.

_____ 10._____ 24. _____ 38.

_____ 11._____ 25. _____ 39.

_____ 12._____ 26. _____ 40.

_____ 13._____ 27.

_____ 14._____ 28.

Name_____ Date _____

Objective: To practice for the *Texas Higher Education Assessment Test*.

Use this answer sheet for the practice test, *Texas Higher Education Assessment Test*, in your textbook. Fill in the correct answer for each numbered item. Be sure to choose only one answer for each numbered item, and fill in the circle completely.

_____ 1. _____ 15. _____ 29.

_____ 2. _____ 16. _____ 30.

_____ 3. _____ 17. _____ 31.

_____ 4. _____ 18. _____ 32.

_____ 5. _____ 19. _____ 33.

_____ 6. _____ 20. _____ 34.

_____ 7. _____ 21. _____ 35.

_____ 8. _____ 22. _____ 36.

_____ 9. _____ 23. _____ 37.

_____ 10. _____ 24. _____ 38.

_____ 11. _____ 25. _____ 39.

_____ 12. _____ 26. _____ 40.

_____ 13. _____ 27.

_____ 14. _____ 28.

Name_____ Date _____

Objective: To gain more practice for the *Texas Higher Education Assessment Test*.

Fill in the correct answer for each numbered item. Be sure to choose only one answer for each numbered item, and fill in the circle completely.

_____1.	_____15.	_____29.
_____2.	_____16.	_____30.
_____3.	_____17.	_____31.
_____4.	_____18.	_____32.
_____5.	_____19.	_____33.
_____6.	_____20.	_____34.
_____7.	_____21.	_____35.
_____8.	_____22.	_____36.
_____9.	_____23.	_____37.
_____10.	_____24.	_____38.
_____11.	_____25.	_____39.
_____12.	_____26.	_____40.
_____13.	_____27.	
_____14.	_____28.	

Name_____ Date _____

Objective: To discover strengths and areas for improvement in reading comprehension and critical reading.

Use this answer sheet for the practice test for *The Master Reader*. Fill in the correct answer for each numbered item. Be sure to choose only one answer for each numbered item, and fill in the circle completely.

_____ 1._____ 15._____ 29.

_____ 2._____ 16._____ 30.

_____ 3._____ 17._____ 31.

_____ 4._____ 18._____ 32.

_____ 5._____ 19._____ 33.

_____ 6._____ 20._____ 34.

_____ 7._____ 21._____ 35.

_____ 8._____ 22._____ 36.

_____ 9._____ 23._____ 37.

_____ 10._____ 24._____ 38.

_____ 11._____ 25._____ 39.

_____ 12._____ 26._____ 40.

_____ 13._____ 27.

_____ 14._____ 28.

Name _____ Date _____

Objective: To discover strengths and areas for improvement in reading comprehension and critical reading.

Fill in the correct answer for each numbered item. Be sure to choose only one answer for each numbered item, and fill in the circle completely.

_____ 1. _____ 15. _____ 29.

_____ 2. _____ 16. _____ 30.

_____ 3. _____ 17. _____ 31.

_____ 4. _____ 18. _____ 32.

_____ 5. _____ 19. _____ 33.

_____ 6. _____ 20. _____ 34.

_____ 7. _____ 21. _____ 35.

_____ 8. _____ 22. _____ 36.

_____ 9. _____ 23. _____ 37.

_____ 10. _____ 24. _____ 38.

_____ 11. _____ 25. _____ 39.

_____ 12. _____ 26. _____ 40.

_____ 13. _____ 27.

_____ 14. _____ 28.

Name_____ Date _____

Scores: % Correct   % Correct

Passage A   _____   Passage E   _____

Passage B   _____   Passage F   _____

Passage C   _____   Passage G   _____

Passage D   _____

The Reading Section of the *Florida State Basic Skills Exit Test* is based on the skills listed below. Circle the number of questions that you missed. Locate pages in your textbook that will help you develop each specific skill. Write out a study plan.

Passage/Question #	Skill
A4, A5, D6, E4, F4, G3	**Determine the meaning of words and phrases.**
AI, A7, CI, D2, EI, E4, GI, G6, FI, F2	**Understand the main idea and supporting details in written material.**
A2, A3, B2, B3, C2, D3, D5, E2, F3, G2, G5	**Identify a writer's purpose, point of view, and intended meaning.**
A6, DI, E3, F5	**Analyze the relationships among ideas in written material.**
B4, C3, D4, G4	**Use critical-reasoning skills to evaluate written material.**
BI, F7	**Apply study skills to reading assignments.**

Plan of Action:

_____

_____

_____

_____

_____

_____

_____

_____

_____

_____

_____

_____

_____

_____

_____

_____

Name_____ Date_____

Scores: % Correct   % Correct

Passage A   _____   Passage E   _____

Passage B   _____   Passage F   _____

Passage C   _____   Passage G   _____

Passage D   _____

The Reading Section of the THEA Test is based on the skills listed below. Circle the number of questions that you missed. Locate pages in your textbook that will help you develop each specific skill. Write out a study plan.

Passage/Question #	Skill
A4, A5, D6, E4, F4, G3	**Determine the meaning of words and phrases.**
AI, A7, CI, D2, EI, E4, GI, G6, FI, F2	**Understand the main idea and supporting details in written material.**
A2, A3, B2, B3, C2, D3, D5, E2, F3, G2, G5	**Identify a writer's purpose, point of view, and intended meaning.**
A6, DI, E3, F5	**Analyze the relationships among ideas in written material.**
B4, C3, D4, G4	**Use critical-reasoning skills to evaluate written material.**
BI, F7	**Apply study skills to reading assignments.**

Plan of Action:

_____

_____

_____

_____

_____

_____

_____

_____

_____

_____

_____

_____

_____

_____

Name_____ Date _____

Scores: % Correct   % Correct

Passage A   _____   Passage C   _____

Passage B   _____   Passage D   _____

The Diagnostic Test for *The Master Reader* is based on the skills listed below. Circle the number of questions that you missed. Locate pages in your textbook that will help you develop each specific skill. Write out a study plan.

Passage/Question #	Skill	Textbook Pages
A6, A7, B7, B8, C1, D5, D6	**Vocabulary**	_____
A1, A8, B2, C2, C4, D1	**Main Idea**	_____
C3, C10, D9	**Supporting Details**	_____
A3, A4, B3, C6	**Thought Patterns**	_____
A5, B5, B6, C5, D7	**Transitions**	_____
A2, A9, C8, C9	**Tone and Purpose**	_____
A9, C7, D8	**Fact/Opinion**	_____
A10, B10, D2, D3, D4	**Inferences**	_____

Plan of Action:

_____

_____

_____

_____

_____

_____

_____

_____

_____

_____

_____

_____

_____

_____

_____

	Score
Chapter 1: A Reading System for Master Readers	
Lab 1.1 Practice Exercise 1	
Lab 1.2 Practice Exercise 2	
Lab 1.3 Review Test 1	
Lab 1.4 Review Test 2	
Lab 1.5 Mastery Test 1	
Lab 1.6 Mastery Test 2	
Chapter 2: Vocabulary Skills	
Lab 2.1 Practice Exercise 1	
Lab 2.2 Practice Exercise 2	
Lab 2.3 Review Test 1	
Lab 2.4 Review Test 2	
Lab 2.5 Mastery Test 1	
Lab 2.6 Mastery Test 2	
Chapter 3: Stated Main Ideas	
Lab 3.1 Practice Exercise 1	
Lab 3.2 Practice Exercise 2	
Lab 3.3 Review Test 1	
Lab 3.4 Review Test 2	
Lab 3.5 Mastery Test 1	
Lab 3.6 Mastery Test 2	
Chapter 4: Implied Main Ideas and Implied Central Ideas	
Lab 4.1 Practice Exercise 1	
Lab 4.2 Practice Exercise 2	
Lab 4.3 Review Test 1	
Lab 4.4 Review Test 2	
Lab 4.5 Mastery Test 1	
Lab 4.6 Mastery Test 2	
Chapter 5: Supporting Details, Outlines, and Concept Maps	
Lab 5.1 Practice Exercise 1	
Lab 5.2 Practice Exercise 2	
Lab 5.3 Review Test 1	
Lab 5.4 Review Test 2	
Lab 5.5 Mastery Test 1	
Lab 5.6 Mastery Test 2	
Chapter 6: Outlines and Concept Maps	
Lab 6.1 Practice Exercise 1	
Lab 6.2 Practice Exercise 2	
Lab 6.3 Review Test 1	
Lab 6.4 Review Test 2	
Lab 6.5 Mastery Test 1	
Lab 6.6 Mastery Test 2	

Chapter 7: Transitions and Thought Patterns	
Lab 7.1 Practice Exercise 1	
Lab 7.2 Practice Exercise 2	
Lab 7.3 Review Test 1	
Lab 7.4 Review Test 2	
Lab 7.5 Mastery Test 1	
Lab 7.6 Mastery Test 2	
Chapter 8: More Thought Patterns	
Lab 8.1 Practice Exercise 1	
Lab 8.2 Practice Exercise 2	
Lab 8.3 Review Test 1	
Lab 8.4 Review Test 2	
Lab 8.5 Mastery Test 1	
Lab 8.6 Mastery Test 2	
Chapter 9: Fact and Opinion	
Lab 9.1 Practice Exercise 1	
Lab 9.2 Practice Exercise 2	
Lab 9.3 Review Test 1	
Lab 9.4 Review Test 2	
Lab 9.5 Mastery Test 1	
Lab 9.6 Mastery Test 2	
Chapter 10: Tone and Purpose	
Lab 10.1 Practice Exercise 1	
Lab 10.2 Practice Exercise 2	
Lab 10.3 Review Test 1	
Lab 10.4 Review Test 2	
Lab 10.5 Mastery Test 1	
Lab 10.6 Mastery Test 2	
Chapter 11: Inferences	
Lab 11.1 Practice Exercise 1	
Lab 11.2 Practice Exercise 2	
Lab 11.3 Review Test 1	
Lab 11.4 Review Test 2	
Lab 11.5 Mastery Test 1	
Lab 11.6 Mastery Test 2	
Chapter 12: The Basics of Argument	
Lab 12.1 Practice Exercise 1	
Lab 12.2 Practice Exercise 2	
Lab 12.3 Review Test 1	
Lab 12.4 Review Test 2	
Lab 12.5 Mastery Test 1	
Lab 12.6 Mastery Test 2	
Chapter 13: Advanced Argument: Persuasive Techniques	
Lab 13.1 Practice Exercise 1	
Lab 13.2 Practice Exercise 2	
Lab 13.3 Review Test 1	
Lab 13.4 Review Test 2	
Lab 13.5 Mastery Test 1	
Lab 13.6 Mastery Test 2	

Practice Tests	
Practice Tests for the *Florida College Basic Skills Exit Reading Test*	
Practice Tests for the *Texas Higher Education Assessment Test*	
Practice Tests for *The Master Reader*	
Skills Awareness Inventory: *Florida College Basic Skills Exit Test*	
Skills Awareness Inventory: *Texas Higher Education Assessment Test*	
Skills Awareness Inventory: *The Master Reader*